SO-BJM-873

MAR 1 4 1994

# HOCKEY!
# The Book for Kids

DISCARDED AND
WITHDRAWN FROM
WARWICK PUBLIC
LIBRARY

WARWICK
PUBLIC
LIBRARY

# HOCKEY

## THE BOOK FOR KIDS

Written by Brian McFarlane
Illustrated by Bill Slavin

J
GV
847.25
M34
1990

KIDS CAN PRESS LTD.
Toronto

Kids Can Press Ltd. acknowledges with appreciation the assitance of the Canada Council and the Ontario Arts Council in the production of this book.

**Canadian Cataloguing in Publication Data**

McFarlane, Brian, 1931 -
  Hockey

Includes index.
ISBN 1-55074-004-0

1. Hockey - Juvenile literature.   I. Slavin, Bill.
II. Title.

GV847.25.M34 1990  j796.96'2  C90-094032-8

Text copyright © 1990 by Brian McFarlane
Illustrations copyright © 1990 by Bill Slavin
Cover illustration copyright © 1990 by Gordon Suavé

All rights reserved. No part of this publication may be reproduced, stored in a retrieval system or transmitted in any form or by any means, electronic, mechanical, photocopying, recording or otherwise except with the prior written permission of Kids Can Press Ltd. or under a licence from the Canadian Reprography Collective.

Kids Can Press Ltd.
29 Birch Avenue
Toronto, Ontario, Canada
M4V 1E2

Edited by Laurie Wark
Book design by N. R. Jackson
Typeset by Alphabets
Printed in Canada

90 0 9 8 7 6 5 4 3

# CONTENTS

CONIMICUT PUBLIC LIBRARY

# ACKNOWLEDGEMENTS

This book is for kids of all ages who love the great game of hockey. Special thanks to former NHL goalie Ken Dryden for his advice and assistance. The professional opinions of fitness expert Al Copetti and nutritionist Fran Berkoff are also much appreciated. Thanks to Valerie Hussey and Ricky Englander of Kids Can Press, and to Laurie Wark, the extremely competent editor, who worked so diligently on the project.

# INTRODUCTION

The world of hockey is an exciting one — it's fast-moving and full of fascinating teams and players. It has teams with astonishing histories, like the Montreal Canadiens, who have captured more Stanley Cups than any club in history. There are legendary players from Gordie Howe — who played as a pro for 32 years and was on the ice playing the night he became a grandfather — to Wayne Gretzky, who has set more records than any player in history.

In this book you'll follow the pros from backyard rinks to the glamorous world of the National Hockey League, and you'll discover:

- tips on how to improve your game
- hilarious hockey history and all about the Stanley Cup
- what a day in the life of a pro is like
- some hockey heroes and all about the player of the decade
- what coaches look for in a player
- and much more.

Did you know that...

- a Chicago Black Hawk player once scored three goals in a mere 21 seconds?
- the Stanley Cup was once kicked into a canal?
- Wayne Gretzky scored 1000 goals in minor hockey by the time he was 13?
- a Canadian team won a game at the world championships by a score of 47-0?

So, whether you're just learning how to skate, you're already on a team, or just a great hockey fan, this book is for you.

P.S. IF YOU COME ACROSS A HOCKEY WORD YOU DON'T UNDERSTAND, CHECK THE GLOSSARY AT THE BACK OF THE BOOK.

# LET'S PLAY HOCKEY

You likely know that the object of the game is to put the puck in the opposing team's net — as often as possible. At the same time, you're trying to keep your opponents from putting the puck in your net.

These basic principles, called offensive and defensive team play, can sometimes baffle the first-time spectator. A newcomer to the sport watches a dozen players whirling around the ice, bumping into each other, chasing after a slippery rubber puck, whipping it occasionally at a well-padded goalie and stopping every few seconds when a whistle blows, sometimes for no apparent reason. Hockey can look like a confusing game at first.

But just as there is always a reason for the whistle to be blown, there are reasons why the players perform as they do. When they fore-check, backcheck, set up plays, change "on the fly," kill penalties and try for power-play goals, they are following a system — a system devised by the coach.

Whether you're new to hockey or just want to brush up on the basics, here's a review that will get you hooked on hockey.

## The ice

An NHL hockey arena or "rink" is approximately 61 m (200 feet) long and 26 m (85 feet) wide. The boards surrounding the rink are topped with shatterproof glass that protects the spectators from flying pucks and sticks.

Five lines are painted on the ice. The goal nets sit on the goal lines — they are painted 3.3 m (11 feet) out from the end boards. The two blue lines divide the rink into three different zones called defensive, offensive and neutral zones. Both ends of the rink can be known as offensive and defensive, depending on the point of view of each team. The end that your own goal net is in is known as your defensive zone and the opposite end is your offensive zone. The centre-ice red line divides the rink in half. The purpose of the lines is to keep the players on the move and to prevent some of them from standing around in front of the opposing goalie waiting for a pass.

There are five large circles painted on the ice. These are used for facing off the puck. During a face-off, only the two players facing off are allowed within the circle.

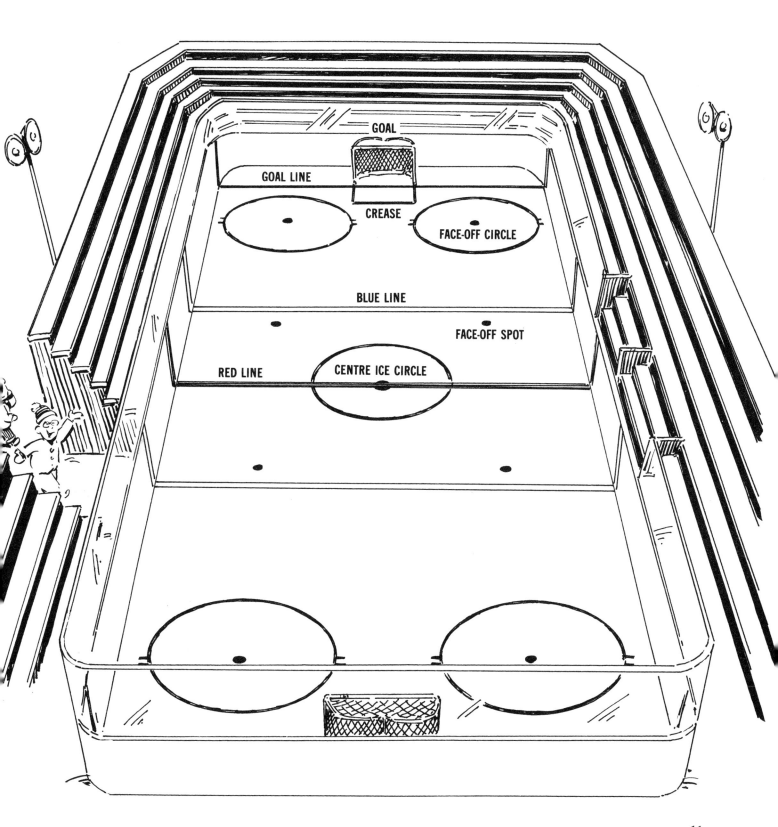

GOAL

GOAL LINE

CREASE

FACE-OFF CIRCLE

BLUE LINE

FACE-OFF SPOT

RED LINE

CENTRE ICE CIRCLE

## Players and playing

The game is divided into three 20-minute periods in the NHL. If the score is tied at the end of the 60 minutes of play, there is a five-minute overtime period, which ends when the first overtime goal is scored. If no one scores in the five minutes, the game ends in a tie.

A professional team consists of up to 20 players. Big-league teams generally carry up to 12 forwards, 6 defencemen and 2 goal tenders, as well as a coach and his assistants, a manager and his assistants, and several trainers, equipment managers and team doctors.

Three forwards play together on a line (left wing, right wing and centre). The centre tries to win face-offs and they all work to set up plays for each other. Forwards must be fast skaters and hard shooters. They try to move the puck — by skating with it, by stick-handling it or by passing it back and forth — into the other team's defensive zone. Their destination is the "slot" (an area directly in front of the goalie). They know that most goals are scored from the slot. From that position, they'll try to beat the goalie with a hard shot — a wrist shot, a slapshot or a backhander — aimed at the corners of the net. Sometimes they try to "deke" the goalie — by faking him out of position — in an attempt to score.

What's the other team doing while this is going on? It is playing defensive hockey. The two defencemen — whose job it is to prevent opponents from scoring — are checking hard in the slot — stickchecking and bodychecking. The defensive team's forwards have come back and they are checking, too. The goalie,

crouched over, will sometimes move out of his net, to "cut down the angles" to the goal, making it very difficult for the attacking team to score.

The puck changes hands frequently, often

several times each minute. If players on the defending team come up with the puck deep in their own zone, they have a break-out play planned — one that gets the puck quickly out of their zone. When that happens, the players on the opposing team rush back towards their zone and play defensive hockey. This is called backchecking.

If players in control of the puck can't organize a break-out play from their own zone, it's often because the opposing team sends speedy forwards in to pressure them. This is called forechecking.

Hockey is so fast that players tire quickly. Remember, they skate in short bursts at speeds up to 50 km/h (30 miles per hour) and they can stay on the ice for only a minute or two. Hockey players often change lines "on the fly" by jumping from the bench to the ice while teammates are jumping from the ice to the bench. In no other sport are players allowed to substitute for others without a break in the action.

The newcomer to hockey will be amazed at the number of plays there are in hockey. The range is almost endless. Some are pre-planned, but many are spontaneous. It takes countless hours of practice — beginning when the player is very young — to become adept at skating swiftly on two thin blades of steel; at manipulating a puck through a defence combination with twists, turns and "dekes"; at sending hard, accurate passes to a fast-skating teammate; at propelling a hard, accurate shot to a corner of the net, especially while being checked with a stick or a shoulder to the body, or fouled by a trip, a slash, a hook or an elbow.

Players and spectators are attracted to hockey by its speed, the thump of body contact, the split-second transition from offence to defence and the fascinating blend of individual performance and disciplined team play.

# GOAL GUARDIANS

Goalies are different from the other players on the ice. Not only do they wear different skates and use different sticks, but they have perhaps the most stressful job on the team. If they make one little mistake that leads to a goal, they'll hear about it from the fans. A good goaltender must be agile and have a sharp eye and excellent reflexes to make all the saves.

Some goalies didn't want to play the position in the first place. As young players, they might have been poor skaters who tried goaltending in order to be on the team. When Georges Vezina, after whom the Vezina Trophy (see page 72) is named, first played hockey, he tended goal wearing his street shoes. He didn't learn how to skate until he was in his teens. But Georges surprised everybody by becoming one of Montreal's greatest goalies. Here are some strange-but-true stories about some other famous goalies.

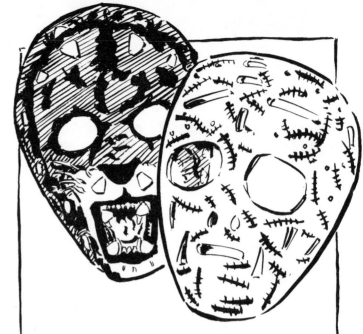

In the 1970s, it was trendy for goalies to wear painted face masks. Gilles Gratton had a ferocious tiger's head painted on his mask to frighten opposing forwards. Gary "Cobra" Edwards had a striking cobra circling his mask, while Gaye Cooley opted for a goal mask with a happy face painted on it. Gerry Cheevers painted marks on his mask to look like the stitches he would have had if the fibreglass hadn't protected him. Today many goalies have their team crests painted on their masks.

Billy Smith of the New York Islanders became the first NHL goalie credited with scoring a goal — although he didn't actually shoot the puck into the opponent's net. He happened to be the last player to touch the puck before an opposing player slapped it into his own team's net. But Ron Hextall was the first netminder to score a legitimate goal. He scored an empty netter against the Boston Bruins in 1988 and a year later scored a play-off goal against the Washington Capitals, also into an empty net. It'll really be one for the record book when a goalie scores on a guarded net!

After Ottawa goalie Percy Lesueur retired in 1916, his family donated his famous goal stick to the Hockey Hall of Fame. Why was it famous? It's the stick he used in every league and play-off game for five straight seasons! Today, goalies often use two or three sticks in one game.

To relieve tension and to keep his mind off the game, goalie Gary Smith would strip off all his equipment between periods of every game. Then he'd promptly put it all back on again. With all that heavy equipment, it must have taken a lot of energy to keep dressing, undressing and dressing again.

It's a wonder Glenn Hall lasted as long as he did in the NHL (18 seasons with Detroit, Chicago and St. Louis). Hall was so nervous he threw up before every game and often between periods. Even so, he set a goalie record that may endure forever by playing in 502 consecutive games.

# Behind the mask

It's difficult to believe that when hockey was first played, goaltenders didn't wear face masks! Even though goalie Clint Benedict wore a primitive face mask for a game or two in 1929, it wasn't until 30 years later that the goalie mask became a permanent part of hockey.

On November 1, 1959, Montreal Canadiens' goalie Jacques Plante was struck in the face by a slapshot during a game in New York. After receiving several stitches, Plante returned to the ice wearing a face mask he'd been using in practices. The mask seemed to give Plante new confidence and the Canadiens embarked on a winning streak. Other goalies followed Plante's smart lead and within a few years all professional goalies were wearing face masks.

Jacques Plante wearing one of his early masks

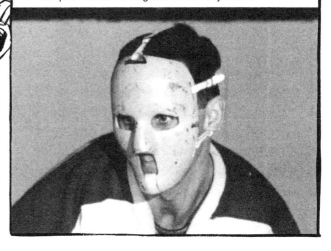

# THE PUCK STOPS HERE

Footballs, baseballs, basketballs, soccer balls, tennis balls and pucks — one of these things is not like the others. Hockey is one of the few sports that doesn't use a ball — and it's the only sport that uses a puck.

Legend has it that the puck was invented one night in the 1800s during a game of shinny. In those days, the players used a hard rubber ball to play, and it frequently flew over the boards and bounced all around the arena. On this night the bouncing ball crashed through an expensive window, and the arena manager grabbed the ball and pared off two sections of it with his jack-knife. He threw the flat centre portion back on the ice and the game continued with the newly shaped object. Because the puck slid along the ice instead of bouncing, it was easier to control and the game became more fun to play, not to mention less dangerous to watch.

Likely no players dread the puck more than goaltenders — especially seeing it go past them. Check out some of these amazing puck stoppers:

• Goalie George Hainsworth of the Montreal Canadiens shut out opposing teams 22 times in the 44-game season of 1928-29. Hainsworth allowed just 43 goals that season, less than one per game. No other goalie has come close to matching his records.

• Terry Sawchuk, who played in the NHL for 20 seasons, finished his career with a record 103 shut-outs.

• Oldtime goalie Alex Connell of Ottawa set an NHL record with six consecutive shut-outs in 1927-28. He played 461 minutes and 29 seconds without allowing a goal.

• Goalie Glenn Hall, while playing for the Chicago Black Hawks, set an amazing record for durability. In the days when NHL clubs employed just one netminder and before goalies wore face masks, Hall played in 502 consecutive games. A neck injury halted his streak in 1962.

## How pucks are made

Millions of pucks are made every year. Huge batches of rubber — enough to make a thousand pucks — are mixed with carbon black (coal dust). The mixture is put in machines that churn out a roll of rubber like a huge sausage. A heavy slicer cuts the rubber into 175-g (6-ounce) pucks (called blanks at this stage), which are placed in moulds. Each mould has cavities to fit 27 blanks. From then on it's like making muffins. Team emblems or logos are glued on the blanks and the moulds are cooked for 20 minutes. To make sure the pucks are shaped perfectly, they're pressed (while cooking) under 900 kg (2000 pounds) of pressure. After that, they are packaged and shipped and ready for NHL stars to take their best shot at them.

## Did you know?

- Pucks are placed in a freezer before big-league games. Frozen pucks slide better and bounce less than non-frozen pucks.
- Some NHL teams use up to 5000 pucks in a season.
- About 30 to 40 pucks are used in most big-league games.
- Hockey leagues have experimented with pucks of different sizes and colours. But they always come back to the black vulcanized rubber pucks that hold their shape and chip less frequently than coloured pucks.

# THE GOAL OF THE CENTURY

If you asked your parents or grandparents to pick the most famous goal ever scored in hockey, do you think they could choose one? Chances are it would be a goal scored on September 28, 1972, in the third period of a thrilling game that had fans on the edge of their seats.

The best players in the NHL formed Team Canada to meet an All Star team from the Soviet Union in what has often been called "The Series of the Century." Almost everyone predicted an NHL sweep of the eight-game series. The Soviet players were considered "amateurs" and they dressed like it — when they arrived in Canada to play the first four games of the series, they carried battered skates and second-rate equip-ment. What's more, their goalie — Tretiak — was said to be very weak, certainly no match for the brilliant stars of Team Canada.

Canadians were in shock when the Soviets won the first game 7-3 at the Montreal Forum. The Soviet players proved to be in peak condi-tion and they could fly! Cana-dian fans breathed a sigh of relief when the Canadians won the second game in Toronto. The third game, played in Winnipeg, ended in a tie but the fourth game in Vancouver was a repeat of game one. Team Canada took too many penalties and lost 5-3. In all of the games, 20-year-old Soviet goalie, Tretiak, was sensational.

Then the teams travelled to Moscow for the final four games. The Soviets won game five and Team Canada's hopes for a series win were fading quickly. One more victory on home ice and the Soviets would be able to claim the series. But the Canadian players gave themselves a pep talk and followed with a spec-tacular rally. Team Canada captured games six and seven by the barest of margins to tie the series. Paul Henderson of the Toronto Maple Leafs scored the winning goal in both games.

But Henderson saved his most dramatic goal for the closing seconds of game eight. Trailing 5-3 in the third period, Team Canada scored twice to tie the game. Then, with just 34 seconds on the clock, Henderson leaped on his own rebound and slipped

the puck past Tretiak. Team Canada won the game 6-5 and captured the most exciting series ever played.

Back in Canada, everyone from the prime minister to the local paper boy stopped what he or she was doing that day to watch the final game on television. And at that moment, with 34 seconds left to play, they'd seen Henderson score hockey's most memorable goal — the goal of the century.

Paul Henderson scores hockey's most famous goal

# WHO INVENTED HOCKEY?

Many hundreds of years ago, long before your great-grand-parents were born, a boy named Hans lived in a small village in Northern Europe. There weren't many roads in the country where Hans lived, but there were lots of waterways. In winter, Hans and his friends would travel along the frozen river from one place to another on handmade skis, snowshoes or skates.

One day, Hans was skating along on his new skates, which were handmade of bone. His father had worked very hard grinding two animal bones until each had a sharp edge — sharp enough to be used as runners to dig into the river ice. Hans hadn't gone far when he almost stumbled over a tree branch. The branch had a crook in one end. He picked it up and carried it with him. He found the branch helped him maintain his balance as he skated swiftly along. Then, ahead of him, Hans noticed a small stone on the ice. Impulsively, he struck the stone with his branch and sent it skimming over the smooth surface. Hey, this was kind of fun!

He skated with the stick and stone until he came upon a group of friends. They began to look for branches with crooks at one end. Soon, they were all pushing stones and pieces of wood across the ice. They agreed with Hans — it was fun. They began to play with just one stone and tried to get it away from each other.

Was this the first game of hockey? It could have been — it resembled a game we know as shinny, which is a crude form of hockey. Hans was likely a Dutch boy — skating was a favourite winter pastime in Holland centuries ago. Even the word skate is said to have come from the Dutch word "schaat." Many old Dutch paintings depict people skating on frozen ponds or canals. Some of them appear to be playing a game somewhat like hockey.

Eventually, iron skate blades replaced the bone or wooden runners that early-day skaters wore. Short sticks, almost like golf clubs, appeared and the disc or ball the players batted over the ice at some time came to be known as a puck.

Although they had skates, sticks and an object to chase, Hans and his friends had few, if any, rules or regulations for their game. There is no record of teams being chosen or such things as goals or goalies, although they may have existed.

It's possible, of course, that other kids just like Hans might have discovered the fun of playing on ice with a stick and a stone long before Hans did. They may have lived in Finland, Norway or Sweden, or perhaps Scotland or England, for skating has a long history in those countries as well. Wherever hockey started, it wasn't long before people were catching on to this exciting winter sport.

21

# HOCKEY COMES TO CANADA

By 1800, people from Northern Europe and the British Isles had settled in Canada. Many of them brought their skates with them and skating soon became everybody's favourite sport during the long Canadian winters.

Soon, our skating pioneers devised a simple game played on ice. It was a team game not unlike the games of shinny we see today. The players set up two goals marked with stones or blocks of wood as goal posts, and players used sticks cut from tree branches. Others used field-hockey sticks brought over from England. The puck was either a ball, a piece of bone or a chunk of wood.

Perhaps the players got the idea for their new game from watching the native Indians play lacrosse. Perhaps the new settlers brought the idea with them, possibly from field

hockey, when they came to Canada. No matter, the best feature of the new game was that it was played on ice. It was fast, it was fun and someone, at some time, began to call it hockey.

Three cities — Halifax, Kingston and Montreal — claim credit for introducing hockey. But the first official hockey game, with written rules to govern the play, was probably played in Montreal in 1875. The rules were drawn up by a group of students at McGill University and these "McGill rules" are the basis for the rules used today.

It wasn't long before every community had an outdoor rink to play on and a team with a strong desire to prove itself against teams from nearby communities. The game soon became so popular across Canada that a governor general, Lord Stanley of Preston, decided to donate a small silver bowl in 1893 to the championship team. The trophy became known as the Stanley Cup and is now one of the most famous trophies in all of sport.

# HOCKEY TALK

Can you figure out what this hockey announcer is saying?

"Mario Lemieux, after winning the draw and deking a defenseman, scored with a backhand drive from the slot. It was upstairs on the power play to complete his hat trick..."

Did you understand what the announcer said? Sometimes it seems like hockey has its own language. Here's the translation: Mario won the faceoff, faked his way past a defenseman and scored his third goal of the game with a high backhand shot from in front of the opposing team's goal while his team held a man advantage because of a penalty.

Here's some more lingo to test your knowledge of hockey talk. (Check the glossary on page 92 for more hockey words.)

**Clearing the puck:** This is the technique of moving the puck away from the net being defended, either toward the side boards, into the corner or up over the blue line.

**Winning the draw:** On a face-off, the player who skates away with the puck or gets it to a teammate wins the draw.

**Head-manning the puck:** This is the technique of passing the puck quickly ahead to a teammate farthest up the ice, making him the head man of the attacking unit.

**Changing lines on the fly:** Each team has three or four forward lines of three players per line. The coach will change these lines every minute or two. One line comes to the bench for a rest while a substitute line takes over the ice. If you're changing lines on the fly, you're changing lines while play is in progress.

**Deking:** When you fake or trick an opposing player or goalie with a clever movement of your body, stick and puck, you are deking. The word deke is thought to be derived from the word decoy.

**Splitting the defense:** When a player with the puck dashes in between two opposing defensemen, he "splits them."

**Getting a hat trick:** When a player pulls a rabbit out of a hat? Not exactly — it's when a player scores three goals in a game. A "pure" hat trick is three consecutive goals by the same player in a game. The expression comes from the fact that years ago, in some sports, a three-goal performer was often presented with a bowler hat.

**Freezing the puck:** Putting the puck in the freezer? Actually, it can mean this — since cold pucks slide better on ice than pucks kept at room temperature, pucks are frozen before each game. Freezing the puck in hockey lingo can also mean to pin it against the boards or net with your stick if you're being checked. Deliberately freezing the puck, or doing it when you're not being checked, can lead to a penalty.

**Ragging the puck:** If you're ragging the puck you're controlling it for several seconds through clever skating and stickhandling. A player may do this to kill off penalty time or to protect a lead late in the game.

**Playing short-handed:** When a penalty is imposed on a player, a substitute is not allowed to take her place on the ice. Her team plays short-handed — a disadvantage until she is released from the penalty box.

**Covering up:** When a player deliberately falls on the puck, that player is covering up. Only the goalie is *legally* allowed to cover up, and he can do it (in his own crease area) only when being checked. Players who fall on the puck to stop play — accidentally or otherwise — risk a minor penalty — even goalies when they are outside their crease.

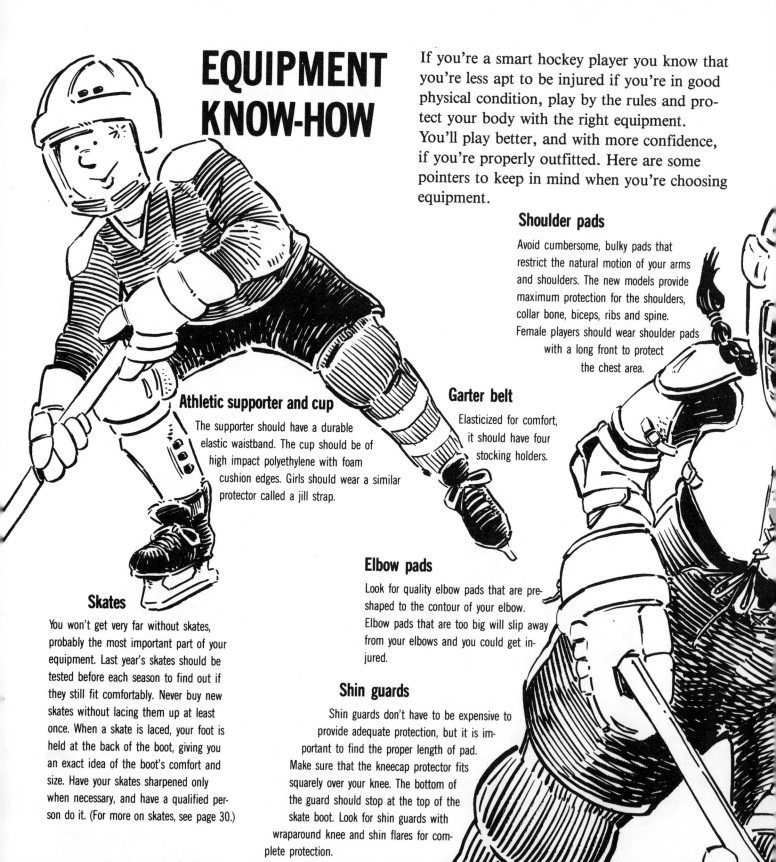

# EQUIPMENT KNOW-HOW

If you're a smart hockey player you know that you're less apt to be injured if you're in good physical condition, play by the rules and protect your body with the right equipment. You'll play better, and with more confidence, if you're properly outfitted. Here are some pointers to keep in mind when you're choosing equipment.

## Shoulder pads

Avoid cumbersome, bulky pads that restrict the natural motion of your arms and shoulders. The new models provide maximum protection for the shoulders, collar bone, biceps, ribs and spine. Female players should wear shoulder pads with a long front to protect the chest area.

## Athletic supporter and cup

The supporter should have a durable elastic waistband. The cup should be of high impact polyethylene with foam cushion edges. Girls should wear a similar protector called a jill strap.

## Garter belt

Elasticized for comfort, it should have four stocking holders.

## Skates

You won't get very far without skates, probably the most important part of your equipment. Last year's skates should be tested before each season to find out if they still fit comfortably. Never buy new skates without lacing them up at least once. When a skate is laced, your foot is held at the back of the boot, giving you an exact idea of the boot's comfort and size. Have your skates sharpened only when necessary, and have a qualified person do it. (For more on skates, see page 30.)

## Elbow pads

Look for quality elbow pads that are pre-shaped to the contour of your elbow. Elbow pads that are too big will slip away from your elbows and you could get injured.

## Shin guards

Shin guards don't have to be expensive to provide adequate protection, but it is important to find the proper length of pad. Make sure that the kneecap protector fits squarely over your knee. The bottom of the guard should stop at the top of the skate boot. Look for shin guards with wraparound knee and shin flares for complete protection.

## Sweater and stockings

They should be light, well-ventilated to prevent heat build-up, resistant to constant abrasion and comfortable. The best stockings have no feet, just a loop that circles the arch of your foot.

## Helmet and mask

Never participate in a game or practice without a helmet and mask to protect your head and face. It's a fact that helmets and masks prevent head and eye injuries. Take time to select a helmet that will give you maximum protection and comfort.

## Gloves

Select gloves with care — you must protect your hands without sacrificing control of your stick. Make certain the thumb area is well protected. When you're testing out gloves, handle a stick while wearing them to get an idea of the stick control they allow.

## Hockey pants

If you are of average build, your hockey pants should be much larger than your waist size. Look for lightweight pants that provide full protection and comfort. Hold your pants in position with a set of adjustable suspenders.

## Hockey stick

When you select a hockey stick, it's important to get the proper lie (the angle between the blade and the shaft) and the proper length. Sawing a bit off a too-long shaft can make a world of difference in controlling the puck. (For more on sticks, see page 38.)

# Did you know?

Hockey was the first team sport to place numbers on the backs of sweaters. It's said that the idea came from Joe Patrick, an organizer of the Pacific Coast Hockey League in 1911. He saw a photograph in a newspaper from England showing a cross country runner wearing a number pinned to his back. Joe thought it was a good idea that should be tried in hockey. His two sons, who ran the Vancouver and Victoria teams, agreed. On opening night of the 1911-12 season, all players in the league wore numbers and within three years, numbered sweaters were adopted by teams in all leagues.

# WEAR NUMBER 13?

Wayne Gretzky always has the right side of his hockey jersey tucked into his hockey pants. In fact, he uses Velcro to make sure it stays there. Former NHL star Butch Goring wore the same battered hockey helmet — the one he first wore in minor hockey — throughout his pro career. And Phil Esposito always wore a black T-shirt under his uniform. Why the strange dressing habits? These players aren't taking any chances with their luck. Once players get into a routine or tradition, they sometimes believe that changing it will bring bad luck. When Wayne Gretzky started playing hockey, he was small for his age and had to tuck his large jersey into his hockey pants — he's been doing it ever since.

Superstitious players always take the same route to the arena and hope that no black cats cross their path. In the dressing room, they cringe at the sight of crossed hockey sticks, and they put their uniforms on in a particular way. Often it's left side first — left skate, left shin pad, left elbow pad and left glove always go on before the right. To do otherwise might bring terrible luck on the ice. Star defence-man Chris Chelios believes it's bad luck to put on his game jersey until all his teammates have theirs on. One of hockey's greatest scorers, Gordie Howe, wouldn't hesitate to

# NOT ME!

borrow a teammate's stick if he thought there were some "lucky" goals in it.

Former Leaf star Darryl Sittler wore his lucky suit and tie before a game one night and scored a record ten points against Boston. He wore the same outfit before a big playoff game with the Philadelphia Flyers and scored five goals in the game — to tie another record. Sittler credits his lucky tie for helping him score the winning goal in overtime against Czechoslovakia in the first Canada Cup series.

Certain players like to follow the goalie onto the ice, others insist on being the last player out. Before the game begins, it's a "must" for some players to tap the goalie on his pads. As for wearing jersey number 13 — forget it. Over the years, only a handful of players has dared to wear that dreaded number. Most feel it could bring instant bad luck.

Hockey players agree it's silly to believe that what they wear to a game or which skate they put on first is going to make a difference in how they play. If they defied tradition and boldly wore number 13, would their legs turn to jelly? Would they suddenly get benched or traded? Of course not, they'll say, but why take a chance?

# IF THE SKATE FITS ...

Do you know why your skate size is often smaller than your shoe size? If you wiggle your toes in your street shoes, chances are your toes don't reach right up to the front of the shoes. But when you slip your foot into a hockey boot, it's important that your toes are right up front. When they are, and you dig in on the ice, you'll get much better leverage. That's why hockey boots are wide in front. And that's why your skates should be a size smaller than your shoes. When you wear a skate that fits snugly, with excellent support in the heel of the boot, you'll skate better without tiring. Follow the pointers on these pages when you're looking for skates.

Take care of your skates. Wipe moisture off them after games and practices. When you take your skates off, unlace them more than halfway down and pull the tongue out, letting air get inside the skate to dry it out. Perspiration from your feet contains body salts that will eat into the skate and eventually damage the lining. So it pays to take care of your skates.

Although some players prefer a leather skate boot, there has been a boom in recent years in moulded boots. Moulded boots have important advantages — they are cheaper and will be warmer for outdoor use.

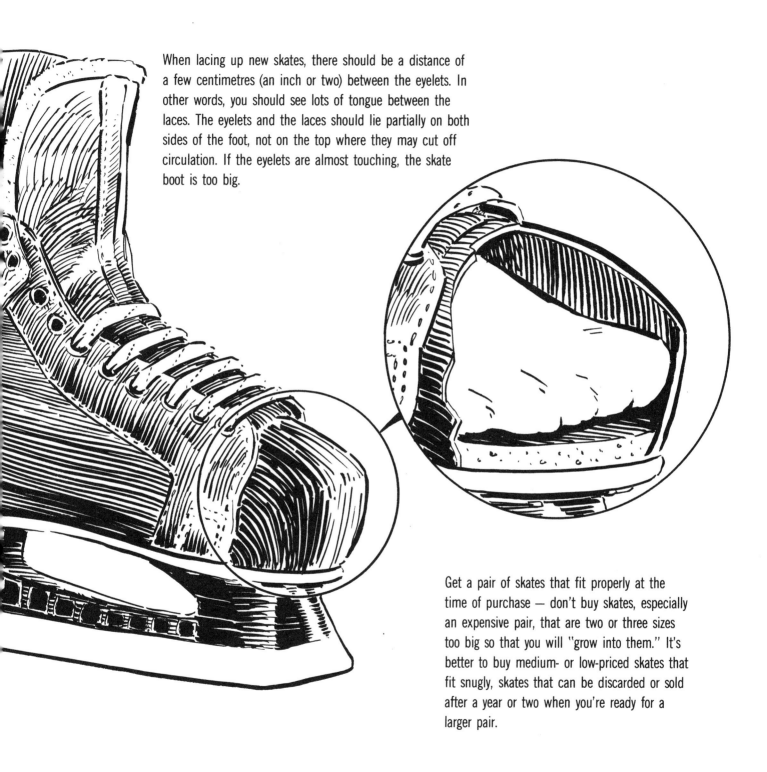

When lacing up new skates, there should be a distance of a few centimetres (an inch or two) between the eyelets. In other words, you should see lots of tongue between the laces. The eyelets and the laces should lie partially on both sides of the foot, not on the top where they may cut off circulation. If the eyelets are almost touching, the skate boot is too big.

Get a pair of skates that fit properly at the time of purchase — don't buy skates, especially an expensive pair, that are two or three sizes too big so that you will "grow into them." It's better to buy medium- or low-priced skates that fit snugly, skates that can be discarded or sold after a year or two when you're ready for a larger pair.

# GET SKATING!

If you want to become a good hockey player, skating is the first and most important skill to master. As you improve, you'll soon develop your own style of skating, but there are a few fundamentals essential to becoming a good skater. Skate with your knees bent and your head up. Lean forward to keep your weight in front of you, and learn to make quick stops and turns. Develop strong leg and hip action, and practise skating forwards and backwards as fast as you can. The better you get, the more fun you'll have playing hockey. Try some of the games on these pages to practise your skating skills.

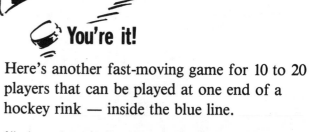

## Hawks and hares

Here's a great game to play with your friends or teammates. It develops speed and agility and is played without using sticks or pucks.

All the skaters (the Hares) but one line up behind the two blue lines, half of them behind each line. The extra player (the Hawk) stands at centre ice. When he shouts "Hawk," all the players must cross to the opposite blue line, trying not to be touched by the Hawk. A skater who is touched by the Hawk also becomes a Hawk and helps to catch the others. The last Hare to be touched is the winner.

## You're it!

Here's another fast-moving game for 10 to 20 players that can be played at one end of a hockey rink — inside the blue line.

All players but one have a puck. The player without a puck is "It." "It" chases the other players and gets a puck away from one of them. "It" must stickhandle with the puck into the goal crease and put the puck in the net. The player who lost the puck tries to steal it back before it enters the crease. If she fails to get the puck back, she joins "It" in another chase for more pucks. The last player with a puck is the winner.

## Heavy Traffic

Here's a game that calls for some fancy stick-handling. It can be played on one-third of a hockey rink, using the two face-off circles and the ice in between them.

The two teams consist of five to ten players each, and each player has a stick and a puck. Each team gathers within its circle and the players stickhandle around without leaving the circle. On a signal, the teams switch circles. Watch out for all those players coming in the opposite direction! The winning team is the one that gets all its players into the other circle first. Each player must be in a stationary hockey stance with a puck on his stick in front of him for the round to be complete. Make it a four-out-of-seven series — like the Stanley Cup finals.

## He shoots, he scores ... backwards?

Cyclone Taylor, playing for Renfrew, Ontario, boasted in 1910 that he could score a goal while skating backwards. In the last game of the regular season, Renfrew blasted Ottawa 17-2. It was in this game that Taylor rushed in on goal, turned around, and with his back to the Ottawa goalie, ripped a hard shot to score in the corner of the net.

# WARM IT UP!

When you see hockey players skating around the rink before a game, they're not just checking out the competition, they're warming up. Your body needs to be warmed up for a game or practice to prepare your muscles for the fast skating, the bumps and falls and shots you'll be taking. Warmup exercises and stretches not only loosen you up, they help you avoid injuries such as muscle pulls or strains. So before you get on the ice, take some time to stretch your muscles, and remember to hold the stretch for at least 15 seconds extending only as far as you feel comfortable. Here are some warmup exercises to try once you hit the ice. Remember, all warmups should be done slowly and repeated several times.

## Kicking the stick

With your hockey stick held in front of you at about shoulder height, lift your right skate to touch the stick while balancing on your left skate. Then repeat the exercise, this time lifting your left skate and balancing on your right. Do this warmup exercise slowly and carefully. As it becomes easier, lift the stick higher, making it a more difficult target. You'll be warming up hamstring, groin and front thigh muscles.

## Stretch the groin

After skating around the ice a few times to loosen up, try gliding along on one skate with the gliding knee bent. Extend the other leg behind you with the foot turned so that your skate blade is flat on the ice. Keep your head up and hold your stick in the same hand as your gliding foot. Use your stick for balance and try to keep most of your weight on the ball of your gliding foot. Now try the same exercise, reversing the position of your feet. This exercise will help prevent groin pulls, a common complaint with hockey players.

## Hamming it up

Glide along on your skates and hold your stick over your head. Then bend over and touch your toes with your stick, keeping your legs slightly bent. You'll feel the stretch in your hamstring muscles, the long muscles in the backs of your legs. Don't lean forward as you bend or you may topple to the ice.

## Hands up for this groin exercise

Skate slowly, feet shoulder width apart, with your hockey stick held in both hands over your head. Spread your legs apart as far as is comfortably possible. Then bend over from the waist, bringing your hockey stick down to your skates. Hold it there. Now bring it back to its original position as you quickly move your feet back to a normal position.

# MAKE YOUR OWN OUTDOOR RINK

Have you ever tried to make your own ice rink and ended up with bumpy slush instead? You may need some co-operation from Mother Nature (the temperature must be well below freezing), but if you follow these steps you should end up with a nice smooth ice surface. Be sure to get permission to make your ice rink before you start.

**1.** Once you've decided on the size of rink you want, make your base on a flat section of lawn. The ideal base is about a 5-cm (2-inch) cover of snow. If your base is more than 10 cm (4 inches), the snow should be packed down — a lawn roller will come in handy for this job. You can make your rink by watering right over the grass, but it may take a little longer. Try using a snow base one year and a grass base the next to see what works best for you.

**2.** Using a snow shovel, build up the sides of the rink with snow.

LAYERS OF ICE →

PACKED SNOW

**3.** Using a garden hose, soak your base with water until it turns into slush. Let it freeze. (Hint: To get a flat surface, take the nozzle off your hose and let the water find its own level. Water back and forth across the width of the rink covering a small area at a time.)

**4.** Keep adding coats of water using a lawn sprinkler, letting each coat freeze before adding another. The best time to water your rink is at night when it will freeze quickly. This may take a few days, but after several sprinklings, you should have a solid sheet of ice.

## Did you know?

One of hockey's greatest performers was born in California. In the 1940s Frank Zamboni, who owned an arena in California, invented a machine to resurface the ice and make it fresh and smooth for hockey players. He called his new invention — you guessed it — the Zamboni! Before the Zamboni came along, teams of arena workers would have to pull large drums filled with hot water around the arena when fresh ice was needed. The drums sat on small carts and released the water through a cloth as they were pulled along — it was a slow process and hard work. The Zamboni works on much the same principle, but it scrapes, cleans and floods the ice in less than ten minutes. Thousands of Zambonis have come out of the California factory, making ice smooth for skaters and hockey players all over the world.

# THE SCOOP ON STICKS

Did you know that hockey players have been playing with wooden sticks for more than a hundred years? Canada's pioneer players made sticks from tree branches, with solid ash a favourite wood. These primitive sticks, patterned after field-hockey sticks, were short and heavy with blades that curved up. Players had to skate crouched over to use them. Finally, someone decided to make lighter sticks with wide blades and longer shafts — so players could skate more easily and shoot the puck harder.

Two-piece sticks (with the blade fitted and glued into the shaft) appeared in the early 1930s and soon the old one-piece models were pushed aside. In the 1970s, laminated sticks (layers of thin strips of wood were glued together to form shaft and blade) were introduced. The first laminated sticks were not always successful. One shipment sent to Western Canada froze in a boxcar, making the glue brittle. When the players used the sticks, they snapped like toothpicks.

Further refinements led to the sticks we use today — 19-ply (19 thin layers of wood) shafts attached to blades that are either one piece or laminated. The latest innovations are sticks with wooden cores reinforced by fibreglass, sticks with aluminum shafts and replacement blades, and the totally synthetic stick. Aluminum sticks are becoming more and more popular in the NHL. They are expensive but the shaft lasts for several months, and a broken blade can easily be replaced. Some NHL players replace 18 to 24 blades a month.

seven-lie stick                five-lie stick                four-lie stick

## Selecting a stick

Wayne Gretzky uses a stick that is light and stiff and has a moderate curve in the blade. He is most concerned about the lie of the stick and the stiffness of the shaft. Tall players, like Mario Lemieux, are more concerned about the length of the stick. Mario uses a 150-cm (60-inch) shaft — the maximum length allowed — and averages one stick per period. Finding a stick that you're comfortable with is very important — here are some tips to help you make your decision.

• Select a stick that suits your stance on the ice. Forget about selecting a stick that comes up to your chin or nose. Decide about stick length when you are on the ice — in your skates. Get a comfortable grip on the stick and then decide on length.

• It's important to get the proper lie (the angle between the blade and the shaft) and the proper length. Most players use sticks with a lie between a four and a seven. A four-lie stick will enable you to carry the puck some distance from your body while a seven-lie stick allows you to carry the puck close to your body. Finding the right lie and length of stick is an individual thing — but very important.

• Experiment with sticks — borrow a team-mate's stick for a few minutes. If it has a shorter shaft or a different curve in the blade, you might find it suits you better than your own. Try different methods of taping a knob on the end of the stick for a better grip.

## How to tape a stick

Once you've decided on a stick that suits you, you'll need to tape it up. You'll find that taping the blade of your stick leads to better puck control. It also helps to keep the blade dry. Begin taping at the heel of the blade and work your way to the end of the blade. One layer of tape is sufficient.

The upper shaft of the stick should be taped so that it can be gripped more firmly. Some players use black tape on the shaft, building up to a little knob. Then they cover the black tape with white tape to protect their gloves from the stickiness of the black tape.

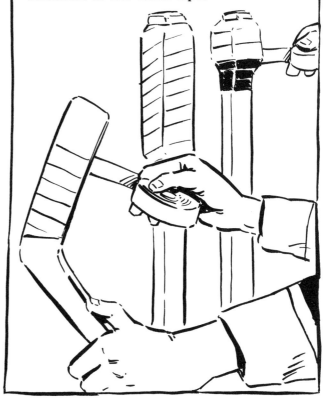

# THE SECRET OF THE STARS

If you think playing hockey is all brawn and no brains, try this experiment with a friend and find out what it really takes. You'll need two pieces of paper, a pen and a stopwatch or a watch with a second hand.

1. Make a list of 20 three-letter words such as toy, ark, box, she.
2. Make a second list using the same words but with the letters all mixed up so that toy becomes yot, ark becomes kra, box becomes xob, she becomes seh, and so on.
3. Ask a friend to read the first list out loud and time her.
4. Ask her to read the second list out loud and time her again. Which time was faster? Why?
   You respond more quickly to familiar patterns.
   What's the point?
   Well, it could have a lot to do with being an expert hockey player.
   To become a good hockey player, you have to do two things. Number one, you have to sharpen your physical skills — skating, handling the puck, checking and so on. Number two, you have to understand that learning to play hockey is just like learning how to read.

Remember the day you picked up your first book? You opened it, and there, staring back at you, was a jumble of squiggles that made no sense. But with practice, you soon discovered that the squiggles formed letters and the letters gathered together to form words. The nonsense turned into sense.

The same thing happens when you watch your first hockey game. All you can see is a bunch of players scattered across the ice, like jumbled-up letters on a page. But the more you watch, the more clearly you pick out how those players are working together as a team. From one set of positions, the players move to another, to another, and another, just like letters rearranging themselves to form different words.

A hockey team can arrange itself into hundreds of patterns during the course of one game. Just as it takes a long time to build up a good vocabulary of words, it also takes a long time to recognize all the patterns in hockey. But once you've learned the patterns, you'll know what to do in every situation — when to pass the puck, when to check an opponent and so on. Even better, you start to anticipate what will happen next.

Practice really does make perfect. Expert hockey players are made, not born. It all goes to show you that in hockey, you have to use your brain as well as your body.

## The family that plays together ...

The Sutter family of Viking, Alberta, holds an unusual record — most brothers in the NHL. Six of seven Sutter brothers — Darryl, Brent, Duane, Brian and twins Rich and Ron — made it to the NHL, and the seventh brother, Gary, almost made it. They could almost form their own team!

# MEET A REFEREE

The unsung heroes of hockey are the referees. The fans never applaud their work, in fact, they often boo them and call them nasty names. But one thing is certain — games wouldn't last very long without referees. They're as essential to the game as the little puck that's shot around. Here's your chance to meet an NHL referee and find out what his job is really like.

**Q. What do you do out there on the ice?**

**A.** I'm in complete charge of the game. I'm responsible for maintaining the flow of the game and I know all the rules inside out. When there's a dispute — and hockey always has disputes — my decision is final.

**Q. Who are the other officials on the ice with you in a game?**

**A.** They are the linesmen — they're my assistants. When the linesmen skate onto the ice before a big-league game they check the goal nets, looking for holes in the netting. When the game begins, they station themselves close to the boards. Each linesman is responsible for half the rink. Most of their time is spent making offside and icing calls, breaking up fights and taking all face-offs except at the start of a period and after a goal. I look after those face-offs. One linesman wears a "beeper" on his belt and when the whistle

stops play, he often gets a signal from the TV truck. That means it's time for a commercial. After 30 seconds, he gets another signal to tell him that the commercial is over and it's time to face off the puck.

**Q. Does anyone else help you out?**

**A.** There are several off-ice officials at every game — the two goal judges, an official scorer, a penalty timekeeper, a game time-keeper and a statistician.

**Q. There sure are a lot of behind-the-scenes people helping out. What do some of them do?**

**A.** The goal judge has an important job — he sits directly behind the goal and keeps his eyes

constantly on the net. If the puck completely crosses the red goal line, he puts on a red light meaning it's counted as a goal for the team that put the puck in the net. Sometimes it is ruled "no goal," but that is for me to decide.

The official scorer keeps track of goals and assists. He is also responsible for obtaining the starting lineup from both clubs before the game. Once the game is over and I sign the official score sheet, no changes regarding credit for goals and assists are permitted.

There's also the statistician who has a complex job that requires good judgement and accuracy. He keeps track of the players on the ice, counts shots on goal and compiles many other statistics that are given to the news media between periods and at the end of the game. Later he forwards all this information to the NHL office.

**Q. What if a player doesn't agree with your decision?**

**A.** If a player gets angry with me and challenges one of my rulings, I may give him a minor penalty, although I will listen to the argument of a team captain or alternate captain. If the player continues to argue, I will give him a misconduct penalty and if he insists on having the last word instead of going to the penalty box, I will hand him a game misconduct penalty, which means he's out of the game.

**Q. How did you learn to be a referee?**

**A.** I started refereeing in minor hockey. One summer I attended a special referees' school to learn more about the business. Then I turned professional and refereed in the minor pro leagues for three seasons. A scout from the NHL — a former referee — liked my work and the next year I was offered a big-league contract.

**Q. Do NHL officials have a training camp each fall — like the players?**

**A.** Yes, we do. At our training camp, we undergo medical and eye tests, take part in early-morning runs, calisthenics and skating drills. We also sit through classroom lectures and we're tested on all the rules. After all that, we choose up sides and have a little fun playing the game. We all love hockey and most of us were pretty good players at one time.

# THAT'S A PENALTY

**Q.:** What's the difference between stickchecking and slashing?
**A.:** A penalty.

Penalties are a necessary part of all body-contact sports like hockey. Referees hand out penalties to keep the game moving and to protect the players from being hurt. If you play hockey, you should avoid getting penalties because you put your team at a disadvantage — your teammates must play on without you while you're in the penalty box. There are several types of penalties in hockey. Can you figure out why the players in the scene were given penalties?

## Minor penalties

When you are given a minor penalty, you must sit in the penalty box for two minutes while your team plays short-handed. If, however, the opposing team scores a goal while you are in the box, you may immediately return to the ice. Minor penalties are handed out for fouls such as tripping, slashing, holding and elbowing.

## Major penalty

If you are caught bodychecking, cross-checking, elbowing, charging or tripping in such a manner that causes an opponent to be thrown violently into the boards, you are given a major penalty and you must sit in the penalty box for five minutes. You must not leave the box until the full five minutes have been served, even if the opposing team scores. In the NHL, when you get a major penalty for causing an injury to a player's face or head, you must pay a $50 fine.

## Misconduct penalty

Using abusive language, banging the boards with your stick, deliberately throwing equipment out of the playing area, or refusing to obey the referee, will get you a misconduct penalty. If you are charged with a misconduct penalty you must leave the game for a period of ten minutes but your team is allowed to substitute for you during that time. In the NHL, a misconduct penalty also brings a fine of $50.

## Game misconduct

If you're charged with a game misconduct penalty, you are suspended for the balance of that game and, in the NHL, fined $200. However, your team may put a substitute on the ice immediately. A game misconduct is automatically given to a player who gets involved in a fight between two other players. It can also be given to a player who has earned a misconduct penalty and continues to behave in the manner that earned him the misconduct penalty in the first place.

## Match penalty

You must leave the game immediately if the referee gives you a match penalty and, in the NHL, pay a fine of $200. A substitute is allowed to replace you on the ice after ten minutes of playing time. A match penalty is imposed on any player who deliberately attempts to injure another player.

## Gross misconduct penalty

It seldom happens, but a referee may impose a gross misconduct penalty on a player, manager or coach, possibly for getting involved physically with the spectators. If you get a gross misconduct penalty in the NHL, you are suspended for the balance of the game, fined $100 and your case is referred to the league president for further disciplinary action.

## Did you know?

• You don't have to be on the ice to get a penalty. If you are sitting on the players' bench and use abusive language to the referee, or if you throw something on the ice, you risk getting a bench minor penalty for two minutes.

• When Tiger Williams retired after 14 seasons, he had spent a record 4421 minutes in the penalty box. That means if Tiger had had to spend his penalty time all at one sitting, he would have spent more than three days in the box.

# ICING AND OFFSIDE

If you are a hockey player or a fan, then you probably know a lot about the rules of the game. You know the game is played on ice by teams of players wearing skates and using sticks to chase after a small rubber puck that they try to propel past an opposing team's goalie. You know each team is allowed six players on the ice at any given time and that players are not allowed to trip, charge, slash, elbow or punch each other. If they do, the referee will send them to the penalty box. But some of the most puzzling rules are those that govern icing the puck and offside.

## Icing the puck

Players who shoot the puck from their own side of the centre-ice line to a point behind the opposing team's goal line are penalized for "icing the puck." When an opposing player touches the "iced" puck, a linesman blows the whistle and the puck is brought back to be faced off near the net of the team that iced the puck. If there was no rule against "icing the puck," a team being outplayed might shoot the puck down the ice at every opportunity. That would be a boring game to watch and play, wouldn't it?

Icing the puck is *not* called if:
• the goalie plays the puck by leaving his net
• the team shooting it is playing short-handed
• one of the opponents is able to reach the puck (in the opinion of the linesman) before it crosses the goal line, but chooses not to in the hopes of getting an icing call.

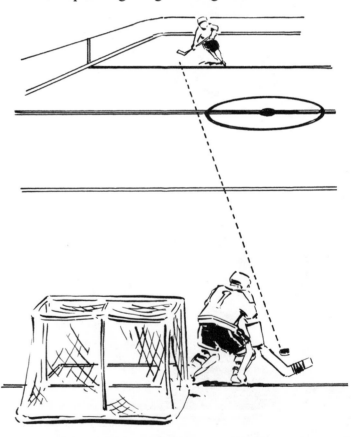

Icing is not called if the goalie plays the puck by leaving his net.

# Offside

The purpose of the offside rule is to prevent one team from sending a player deep into the opposing team's zone to wait for a long pass and gain an unfair advantage.

A player is offside when:
- the puck crosses her opponent's blue line after she does
- she takes a pass that started behind her own blue line, when she is beyond the centre-ice line

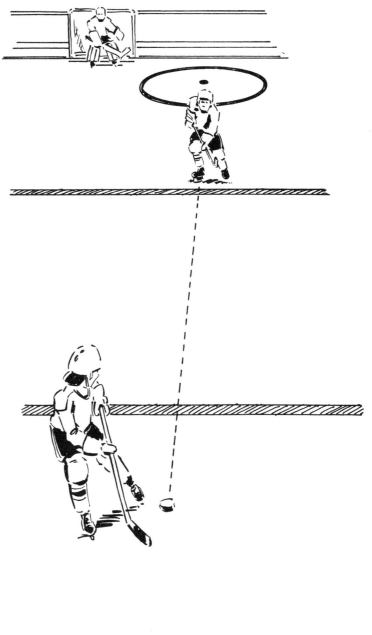

An offside by the attacking team. The pass receiver's skates are over the blue line.

An offside from the defensive zone. Puck crosses two lines to a receiver.

# GREAT MOMENTS IN HOCKEY

Like any exciting, fast-moving sport, hockey has many high-lights and memorable moments. Here are just a few of the classics.

## A memorable hat trick

It was the final game of the 1951-52 season and the Chicago Black Hawks were playing the New York Rangers in New York. The Hawks were trailing in the third period when suddenly, a speedy Hawk forward named Bill Mosienko caught fire. He scored on rookie goalie Lorne Anderson at 6:09, 6:20 and 6:30 — three consecutive goals in 21 seconds. The Hawks won the game 7-6 and Mosienko established a record that has lasted for decades.

## McGee was a mighty scorer

The greatest single-game scoring outburst by any player in history took place long before Darryl Sittler, Mike Bossy, Wayne Gretzky or Mario Lemieux came along. Frank McGee, who played for the Ottawa Silver Seven shortly after the turn of the century, ripped 14 goals past 17-year-old Albert Forrest, goalie for the Dawson City team in a Stanley Cup match played in 1905.

## Sittler's big night

On the night of February 7, 1976, at Maple Leaf Gardens, the Toronto Maple Leafs were playing the Boston Bruins. The Leafs' captain, Darryl Sittler, was facing a rookie goalie, Dave Reece. The young Bruin netminder's big-league career came to an abrupt end after Sittler blitzed him for six goals and four assists in the game. Sittler became the first NHL player to collect ten points in a single NHL match.

## Clancy's busy game

King Clancy once played every position, including goal tender, in a Stanley Cup game for
the Ottawa Senators in 1923. He played right
and left defence and took a turn at all three
forward positions. Then, when Ottawa goalie
Clint Benedict was penalized (in those days
goalies had to serve their own penalties), he
handed his goal stick to Clancy. Clancy took
over in goal and held the opposition scoreless
until Benedict returned. Clancy was just as
versatile off the ice — he went on to be a
coach, referee and hockey executive too.

## Mr. Sudden Death

When Mel Hill started playing with the Boston
Bruins in 1937-38, he scored a mere ten
regular season goals that year, but when the
play-offs began, he stood out like a beacon.
The Bruins met the New York Rangers in the
first round and Hill scored the winning goal in
overtime in game one. In game two, he scored
again in overtime to give the Bruins their
second straight triumph. Then, in game three,
Hill did it again. He whacked in another overtime goal. The Bruins went on to win the
Stanley Cup, and Hill promptly earned the
nickname "Sudden Death" Hill.

# HE SHOOTS! HE SCORES!
# (Tips from a pro)

Hi, hockey fans! Welcome to our intermission show. Tonight on *Brian Talks Hockey*, we're going to talk about what it takes to score goals. We've got an expert here with us tonight, Brett Hull. Brett has scored a lot of goals already in his career and has one of the hardest shots in hockey.

**Brian: Brett, you've scored a lot of goals with your shot. What makes you such a good shooter?**

**Brett:** You know what they say, Brian — practice makes perfect. So I get lots of practice. I love to shoot the puck, so practising my shots is never a chore, it's fun.

**Brian:** Well, good shooters seem to run in your family — your father, Bobby Hull, was famous for his hard, accurate shot. I'm sure our viewers would like to know your secret, Brett. How do you shoot the puck?

**Brett:** If I'm carrying the puck in on goal, I cradle it with my stick — with the puck somewhere in the centre of the blade. I can always tell when the puck is in the right spot — I can feel it in my hands. Then I'm ready to take my shot. With my head up, I can see the mesh in behind the goalie. That's what I want to hit, the place where the goalie's not. I don't have to look down at the puck because I know where it is on my stick. With a sweeping motion, and using lots of wrist and arm action, I shoot for an opening. I'm a right-handed shooter so most of the power for the shot comes from my right leg and foot.

**Brian:** Let's take this step by step. What about the position of your hands when you're shooting?

**Brett:** Before I shoot, I shift my hands to a position most comfortable to me. Not too far apart or I won't get enough flexibility or whip in the stick. Not too close together or I won't get enough power from my lower hand. I've learned the best hand positions for me through trial and error. Most players learn that way.

**Brian:** What about following through on your shot?

**Brett:** Follow-through is very important. Some young players think the shot is over once the puck leaves their stick. Good shooters get hard, accurate shots when they follow through until the stick blade is pointing towards the target.

**Brian:** Do you use a different technique on slapshots?

**Brett:** It's pretty much the same technique with a couple of exceptions. When you pull your stick back for a slapshot, you must know where the puck is on the ice. Take a quick look down as you wind up for the shot, so you'll know where to make contact. Also, grip the shaft of the stick a little tighter because you don't want the blade to

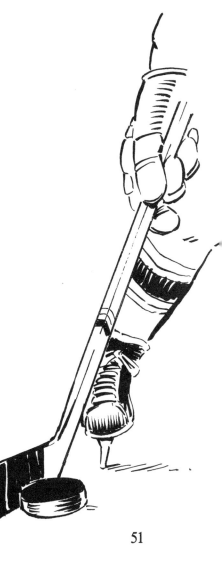

turn in your hands when you strike the ice and the puck. When I release a slapshot, I get my full weight into it — I use my legs, wrists, shoulders and back to power the puck towards the net.

**Brian: Do you know when you shoot the puck that it is going to go in the net?**

**Brett:** Sometimes. But remember, NHL goalies are very quick and very clever. Often you think you've got a sure goal and the goalie makes a fantastic save. Other times you just know the puck is going in. For example, if the goalie makes the first move, I'm confident I can beat him — most of the time, anyway. If he stands up and holds his ground, forcing me to make the first move, then it's more difficult for me to score. Then I have to hit an opening, I have to be more accurate. Remember, it's easier to beat a goalie if you can get him to move first.

**Brian: How much time do you take to get your shot away?**

**Brett:** Not much. Sometimes just a split second, especially when I'm in the slot and there's an opposing player coming at me. I know if I don't get my shot away quickly, I'm not likely to score. That's when I rely on strong wrist and shoulder action to get the shot away because there's no time to throw your full weight into the shot. And often there's no time to judge where the corners of the net are or where the goalie has positioned himself so you just blast away, hoping to catch an opening.

**Brian: What do you do immediately after you shoot?**

**Brett:** Well, I've learned not to stand there admiring my shot. I've learned how important it is to barge in and look for a rebound. Sometimes a player is so positive the puck is going in the net that he'll start to raise his arms to celebrate a goal. Then the goalie makes a miraculous save and the rebound comes right out at your feet. Nobody looks more foolish than a player who's got his arms in the air while the puck is bouncing around at his feet.

**Brian: That's for sure! Thanks for those great tips, Brett. I'm sure all the young players watching tonight will try them out. That's our show for tonight, in a moment, the play-by-play of the second period.**

# Speedy scoring records

• Nels Stewart of the Montreal Maroons scored a record two goals in four seconds against the Boston Bruins in 1931.

• Montreal's great scorer, Rocket Richard, once earned all "three stars" following a hockey game at the Montreal Forum. Richard scored all five goals in a 5-1 victory over Toronto. After the game, Richard was given a standing ovation when he was introduced as star number one, star number two and star number three.

• Toronto Maple Leaf rookie Gus Bodnar amazed everybody in the opening game of the 1943-44 season. Bodnar scored a goal against the New York Rangers on his first NHL shift — just 15 seconds after the opening whistle. It's a rookie record that still stands.

• Bryan Trottier of the New York Islanders and Doug Smail of the Winnipeg Jets share a record for the fastest goal from the start of a game. Each player scored after just five seconds of play.

# WHAT COACHES LOOK FOR

Do you ever wonder what your coach sees in you? Does he think you're a smart player with the puck? Does he like your attitude? Why does he play you on defence instead of on one of the forward lines? And why does he like to have you on the ice during a power play? What does a coach look for in a player anyway?

No matter what the level of hockey — pee wee to pro — coaches look for disciplined players and players with lots of skills. All coaches rate skating as an important skill. Without good skaters, a team is not likely to be successful. Shooting, passing, checking and stickhandling skills are also important if you hope to play junior, college or professional hockey. Good coaches can teach these skills, but it's up to the player to master them. If you play hockey, you may have many coaches over the years. Each one will be different and will have his own coaching style and philosophy. Try to conform to your coach's style, and learn as much as you can from all of your coaches.

Most coaches have some sort of plan in organizing a team. A good coach will try to place the players in the positions on the ice that suit them best and he will have definite ideas of how the team should forecheck, backcheck and kill penalties. One skill that coaches often look for in a player is checking. Many players are strong offensively — they can shoot and score goals — but they have never concentrated on checking. The success of a team will often depend on skilful checking, so the sooner you learn the skills of checking the better.

## Bodychecking

To be a good checker, it is not necessary to hand out bruising bodychecks. It's often enough to stay close to the player you're checking, to bump him slightly with your body and knock the puck away with your stick. It's important to learn how to check without drawing penalties.

## The sweep check

The sweep check is an attempt to sweep the puck away from your opponent. It is done with a sweeping motion of the stick held in one hand. It is a well-timed slap at the puck to jar it loose from your opponent's stick.

## The poke check

The poke check, like the sweep check, is used to knock the puck away from your opponent. It is a quick, one-handed thrust forward, aimed at the puck or stick blade of your opponent. Defencemen find the poke check particularly useful.

## Forechecking

If you go into the offensive zone after an opposing player who has the puck, you're forechecking. Only one attacking player forechecks while a linemate gets ready to pick up the loose puck. The most important thing in forechecking is to take the puck carrier out of the play. Try to force him close to the boards by skating towards him at an angle. If you skate straight at him, he can move either to his left or his right.

## The stick lift

Simply catch up to the puck carrier and lift her stick by placing your stick under hers and raising it. Once her stick is raised, try to scoop the puck away from her.

## Backchecking

You must learn to come back when the other team is on the attack. Stay between your opponent and the puck. If he gets the puck, try one of the stick checks or use your body to take him out of the play. When possible, rub him along the boards with a shoulder check, forcing him to give up the puck.

# SCORING GOALS (Tips from a coach)

"You can't score if you don't shoot the puck."

How often have you heard that from your coach? Shooting is something you should practise whenever you get a chance. Most pros shoot the puck well because they work on their shot at every opportunity. When they were young, they may have shot a ball against a garage door, or fired away at a board or canvas target set up in the backyard. Here are some drills you can try to help you score more often. With practice, you'll turn your "close calls" into "sure things" and make that red goal light flash.

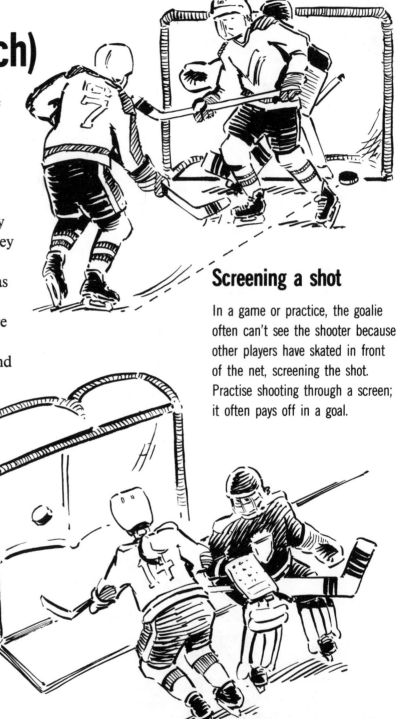

## Screening a shot

In a game or practice, the goalie often can't see the shooter because other players have skated in front of the net, screening the shot. Practise shooting through a screen; it often pays off in a goal.

## Watch the goalie

If the goalie stands back in her net, common sense tells a forward to shoot for the openings. If the goalie moves out in front of the crease, she cuts down the angles to the net, making it more difficult to score. A shooter moving in on the goalie will find her easier to deke if she's well out of her net, so keep an eye on what the goalie's doing.

56

## Tip the puck in

Stand off to the side of the net and pass the puck back to your defenceman. When he shoots at the net, use the blade of your stick to change the direction of the shot, tipping the puck past the goalie. Try to deflect the puck to the corners of the net and through the goalie's legs.

## Passing, shooting and scoring

Stand in front of the goalie and have a teammate send you good, hard passes. If possible, shoot the puck without having to stop it first. Aim for the corners of the net. Occasionally try to shoot the puck between the goalie's legs.

# Off-ice shooting

You can practise shooting when you're not on the ice by making your own hockey target board. Paint circles on your board or get an adult to help you cut four corner holes in a piece of plywood and set it up against a wall or backyard fence. Use a piece of Masonite or some other smooth surface as a platform from which to shoot the puck. Now see how often you can hit the targets. Try moving the board farther away or closer to you. Challenge your friends to a shoot-out and see who can score the most goals.

# GIRLS IN HOCKEY

The next time Team Canada wins an Olympic hockey championship, don't be surprised if a team of women comes home wearing the gold medals. Girls' hockey is growing in popularity — there's a new wave of young women playing the game. They are playing with skill and enthusiasm, but female players are no longer satisfied just playing league games and taking part in occasional tournaments. They have a much bigger goal in mind — an Olympic setting for their game.

The first women's world championship, played in 1990 in Canada and won by the Canadian team, has convinced Olympic organizers to think seriously about adding women's hockey to their schedule of events — initially as a demonstration sport. There are already at least eight nations eager to compete.

But what about professional hockey? Why doesn't a woman play centre ice for the Edmonton Oilers? Or tend goal for the Montreal Canadiens? One reason is the way men and women are built.

Adult men have more muscle and are, on average, larger than women. As a result, men are good at sports where strength and size are a factor. Women have more body fat and tend to be smaller than men, which makes them better at sports that require endurance, like long-distance swimming or running. Of course there are always exceptions, and men and women can both play all sports, but it becomes difficult to compete together in some

A ladies' hockey team of 1910

sports, like hockey and long-distance running, where body build, size and endurance are factors.

This difference in build between males and females isn't noticeable until about the age of 12, when kids' bodies begin to change. That's why girls under 12 who play on boys' hockey teams are right at home. When the boys develop more muscle, height and weight, girls begin to join all-women leagues.

Some female players look to boys' leagues for their challenge. You may have heard about some girls who have taken their cases to court in an effort to be allowed to play along with the boys.

Susie Levy is a member of the Chicago Dragons men's amateur hockey team and she is quoted in *New Woman* magazine as saying:

"If what I do says anything to other women, especially young girls, it is that you can do anything you want to if you're willing to work hard at it and persist. Seek out the opportunities wherever they may be. Hockey was my dream and I did everything I could to get to where I am today."

Although there's a new look to women's hockey, and a bright future, interest in the game among young women is nothing new. Organized women's hockey games were being played as long ago as 1890. Intercollegiate hockey for women was very popular in the early 1900s, too. Can you imagine your great-grandmother playing hockey in a long skirt and a bulky sweater, while wearing a stocking cap and figure skates? Or in the bloomers that were common by 1918? It's quite a contrast to the female player of the 1990s — gone forever are the white figure skates girl players once wore. The picks in the blades were definitely unsuited for hockey.

But the future of women's hockey belongs to young players and fans like you and 12-year-old Samantha Holmes, who are working to build the status of their sport.

Samantha wants the chance to compete in hockey with other countries from all over the world. She has written letters to everyone from her local member of Parliament to the president of the International Olympic Committee in an effort to promote hockey for girls. Can her dream of participating in the Olympics be too far away?

## Kid power!

Samantha Holmes wanted a better future for women's hockey. Here's a letter she wrote to the International Olympic Committee when she was ten years old:

Dear Sir or Madam,

I am ten years old and have played hockey for five years. I am quite a good player and was just picked as one of the top ten female hockey players in Mississauga.

Three weeks ago I visited Calgary and attended six Olympic hockey games. I did not see any women's hockey. When I get older I want to be able to compete in hockey with other countries all over the world. Will I have that chance? If not, please let me know why, and I will try to understand. If the answer is no, what can you do to change that? I don't want to give up my dreams.

I thank you very much for reading my letter. I hope that you will take the time to answer this letter, because it means everything in the world to me.

Sincerely,
Samantha Holmes #7

Samantha Holmes posing for a pre-game shot

# Abby Hoffman's hockey secret

When Abby Hoffman played hockey with her brothers down at the corner rink, she figured she was just as clever on skates as the boys her age. So in 1955, eight-year-old Abby signed up as a player in the Toronto Hockey League as Ab Hoffman, defenceman. And what a player Ab turned out to be! Late in the season, the league selected an All Star Team and Ab Hoffman was named one of the best defencemen. However, a routine check of Ab's birth certificate revealed something very strange — ''he'' was listed as a female!

Suddenly, Abby's secret was out — she became an instant celebrity. Her photo and her story were in all the papers. She was interviewed on radio and television. She received invitations to see NHL games at the Montreal Forum and Maple Leaf Gardens. Nobody tried to bar her from hockey and she played another year with the boys. Then she decided to give girls' hockey a try. In the girls' league she was outstanding — the most talented young woman on the ice.

Eventually, Abby left hockey and went on to excel in other sports, first swimming, then track and field. In time, she became a world-class runner and competed for Canada in two Olympic Games. But she'll always be remembered as the first girl hockey player to create a sensation by starring in an all-boys' league. Her unique story inspired countless other girls to get involved in hockey.

# HOCKEY HEROES

Who's your favourite hockey player? There's probably at least one player you like to watch more than the others. But what would you say if I asked you who's the greatest hockey player of all time? That's a little trickier — hockey has produced many great stars over the years. Here are just a few of the best on ice — hockey heroes who've become legends in the game.

## Gordie Howe

Gordie Howe is the only player in history to play during five decades. His endurance may never be matched. Howe played professional hockey for 32 seasons from 1947 to 1980 and led the Hartford Whalers in scoring in 1977-78 with 96 points — as a 50-year-old grandfather. During his amazing career in two pro leagues, he scored 1071 goals. Howe is the only player to play with his own sons in pro hockey (with Hartford in the NHL and with Houston in the WHA) and he's the only player to have his sweater number retired by two NHL teams. The Detroit Red Wings, his original NHL team, retired his famous number 9 in 1972, the year he was inducted into the Hockey Hall of Fame. His Hartford Whalers number 9 was retired on Gordie Howe Night, February 18, 1981.

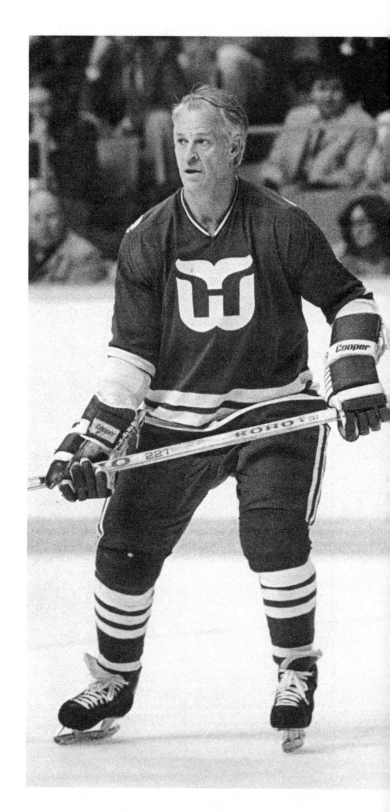

## Maurice (Rocket) Richard

Flashy right-winger Maurice Richard of the Montreal Canadiens was a hot-tempered player who took off like a rocket whenever he had the puck. He was the first NHLer to score 50 goals in 50 games. He was noted for his clutch goals and for many years, he held the record for career play-off goals. During his 18-year career in Montreal, he scored 544 goals in 987 league games.

## Bobby Orr

When 18-year-old Bobby Orr joined the Boston Bruins, they quickly rose to the top of the league standings and won two Stanley Cups. He played for the Bruins in the 1970s and Boston coach Don Cherry called him the greatest player who ever lived. Orr's chronic knee problems forced him from the game in 1979 at the age of 30. Orr won the Norris Trophy as top defenceman a record eight times in a row and the Art Ross Trophy as the NHL's scoring champion. No defenceman had ever won a scoring title prior to Orr and he did it twice. He won the Lou Marsh Trophy in 1971 as Canada's outstanding athlete and the Lester Patrick Trophy for outstanding service to hockey.

63

## Ken Dryden

When he was called up from the minors to tend goal for the Montreal Canadiens late in the season of 1971, Ken Dryden became an instant star. He led Montreal to the Stanley Cup that year and became the series MVP. And, he didn't stop there — the following year he won the Rookie of the Year award. Then, prior to the 1973-74 season, the 26-year-old netminder announced his retirement from hockey. Ken was ready to pursue the career he had studied for at Cornell and McGill Universities — he became a lawyer.

But the Canadiens wanted him back, and he signed with them again the following year,

## Bobby Hull

Early in his NHL career with the Chicago Black Hawks, Bobby Hull's blond good looks earned him the nickname "The Golden Jet." Young fans loved him because he always had time for them and signed autographs endlessly. Hull's sizzling slapshot — timed at 190 km/h (118.3 miles per hour) — terrified goalies and he was the first NHL player to score more than 50 goals in a season. In 16 NHL seasons, Hull scored 610 goals. In 1972, he helped launch the World Hockey Association and signed hockey's first million-dollar contract.

doubling his previous big-league salary. Ken Dryden went on to become the greatest goalie of his time. When he retired for good in 1979, he was six-time Stanley Cup winner with the Canadiens, he had won the Smythe Trophy, the Calder Trophy and the Vezina Trophy (five times) and had played with Team Canada several times. He has since been inducted into the Hockey Hall of Fame, and continues to pass on his passion for the sport to Canadians through the books he has written and through his continuing enthusiasm for hockey.

## Guy Lafleur

The scoring star who led the Montreal Canadiens to four Stanley Cups in the 1970s was Guy Damien Lafleur, a swift and graceful right winger who had once scored 130 goals in a single season with his junior team, the Quebec Remparts. The top NHL draft pick in 1971, Lafleur was under great pressure to become an instant superstar and he struggled early in his career. In 1974-75, he finally blossomed and during his glory days with the Canadiens, Lafleur recorded six consecutive 50-goal seasons and won three scoring titles and two Hart Trophies as the league's MVP (most valuable player). A long scoring slump prompted his retirement during the 1984-85 season and he was out of hockey until the 1988-89 season, when he made a comeback

with the New York Rangers. His return made him only the second player in history (Gordie Howe was the other) to play in the league after being voted into the Hockey Hall of Fame. In 1989, Lafleur joined the Quebec Nordiques, returning to the city where he was idolized as a junior 20 years earlier.

# PLAYER OF THE DECADE

No matter who your favourite player is, Wayne Gretzky is likely on your list of all-time greats. In the history of the NHL, no player has been so popular or so admired as Gretzky. He began his professional career at age 17 with the Indianapolis Racers of the World Hockey Association where Wayne's hockey income jumped from $25 a week to $3000 a week with the Junior A Sault Ste. Marie Greyhounds. Wayne was on his way!

By age two, Wayne was skating on a backyard rink his father built and at five he joined his first team, the Nadrofsky Steelers. He scored one goal that season.

As a ten year old, Wayne's scoring touch began to attract a lot of attention. He scored an astonishing 378 goals in 85 games. At the Quebec Pee Wee Tournament one year, he scored 23 points in five games to break a record set by Guy Lafleur and on April 10, 1974, two months past his 13th birthday, Wayne scored his 1000th goal in minor hockey. He moved to Toronto to play Junior B hockey with the Young Nationals and was named the league's outstanding rookie. The following season he joined Sault Ste. Marie and was again named rookie of the year.

When he turned pro with the World Hockey Association at the age of 17, he was labelled "too young and too skinny" by some scouts. He fooled them all. Scoring 46 goals, he finished third in WHA scoring and once more captured rookie-of-the-year honours. During his initial WHA season, his contract was purchased by the Edmonton Oilers.

Gretzky with the L.A. Kings

Gretzky (in the white gloves), age 10

When Edmonton and three other WHA teams joined the NHL in 1979, Wayne was ready for the stiffer competition. At 19, he became the youngest player to score 50 goals in a season and he was named the league's most valuable player. Then followed seasons when he scored 92 goals (76 was the previous record) and 212 points, both marks thought to be unreachable in an 80-game schedule. And best of all, four Stanley Cups went to the Oilers during the decade of the 1980s.

The numerous scoring records, all the trophies and awards achieved by Wayne were mind-boggling. There had never been such a record-setter. He became the game's brightest, most sought-after star.

One man who sought him was the new owner of the Los Angeles Kings, and he was willing to pay big money to get Gretzky. In 1988, the greatest trade in hockey history rocked the sports world. Wayne Gretzky was going to play for the Los Angeles Kings. Gretzky quickly brought sellout crowds to the Los Angeles Forum and he helped move the Kings from 18th to 4th place in the overall NHL standings.

Early in the 1989-90 season, when he scored his 1851st point, Wayne passed Gordie Howe as the top scorer in NHL history. It took Howe 26 years to set the standard. Wayne surpassed it in his tenth season.

As one of hockey's living legends, under constant pressure to produce more goals, more wins and make more personal appearances, how does Wayne deal with the stress? Where does he go to get away from it all? He says it's where he's always been most comfortable — on the ice.

# Did you know?

• To average a goal a game over an 80-game schedule was once thought to be impossible. Wayne Gretzky did it twice. In the 1981-82 season he scored 92 goals (in 80 games), and in the 1983-84 season he scored 87 goals (in 74 games). Mario Lemieux, in the 1988-89 season, became the second NHL player to average more than a goal a game in one season. He scored 85 times (in 76 games). In the 1990-91 season, Brett Hull scored 86 goals (in 78 games).

• Oldtime star Joe Malone scored 44 goals in just 20 games during the NHL's first season in 1917-18. No other player in history — not even Gretzky — has averaged more than two goals per game.

# THE STANLEY CUP

Did you know that the Stanley Cup is the oldest team trophy competed for in North America? The trophy has been the ultimate goal of every worthy hockey team in North America, amateur and pro, for almost a hundred years. Over the years, teams from 17 different leagues have competed for the Cup. When Canada's governor general, Lord Stanley of Preston, donated the Cup in 1893 to the championship team of Canada, he really started something.

The first team to win the Stanley Cup was from the Montreal Amateur Athletic Association. There was no play-off system that first year so the Montrealers, with a 7-1 record, were simply handed Lord Stanley's brand new trophy. And what a small trophy it was — a silver bowl about the size of a football and worth about $50.

There was no real challenge for the Cup until the following year, when there were two challenges. First, the Montreal Amateur Athletic Association team beat the Montreal Victorias 3-2. That was the first Stanley Cup play-off game and it attracted a huge crowd of 5000 noisy fans. A few days later, Ottawa challenged the Montreal A.A.A. team. Montreal's Billy Barlow, the earliest Stanley Cup hero, scored twice as Montreal won 3-1 and the engraver rushed off to engrave the names of the victorious players on the Stanley Cup.

It wasn't long before hockey teams everywhere in Canada were scrambling after the Cup. Challenges came from places like Winnipeg, Manitoba, Rat Portage, Ontario and New Glasgow, Nova Scotia. The most incredible challenge for the Cup came in 1904 from Dawson City in the Yukon. The Dawson City players travelled 4000 miles by bicycle, dogsled, steamship and train to challenge the Ottawa Silver Seven for Lord Stanley's trophy. Unfortunately, the Dawson City team didn't win the trophy — in fact, they lost by the biggest score ever in Stanley Cup play. The scores were 9-2 and 23-2. In the second game, Ottawa star Frank McGee scored a record 14 goals.

Today, the Cup is under the exclusive control of the NHL. Perhaps someday the NHL will accept a Stanley Cup challenge from the Soviets, the Czechs or some other hockey-mad nation. If it does, there's one more great adventure ahead for Lord Stanley's famous trophy.

# Unusual Stanley Cup games

## Longest overtime ...

A game that kept the fans up half the night, and on the edge of their seats, was played in Montreal in 1936. That night the Montreal Maroons and the Detroit Red Wings staged a tremendous battle through 116 minutes and 30 seconds of overtime before Detroit's Modere (Mud) Bruneteau scored the winning goal in a 1-0 victory. The game was settled in the sixth overtime period — the longest overtime in Stanley Cup history.

## Shortest overtime ...

Some fans were still strolling back to their seats and missed the shortest overtime in Stanley Cup history. When the Calgary Flames faced the Montreal Canadiens in game two of the 1986 finals, the Canadiens' Brian Skrudland scored the winning goal after a mere nine seconds of overtime — a play-off record.

# STANLEY CUP ADVENTURES

If the Stanley Cup could talk, you might find some of the stories it would tell hard to believe. In the past, it's been treated badly, as if no one cared for it. But every year at play-off time, players think of little else but winning it. Chances are no other trophy has been hugged and kissed and photographed more often.

## The Cup gets the boot

After a Stanley Cup victory party in 1905, the Ottawa champions started homeward. As the players passed the frozen Rideau Canal, one of them dared another to show off his football form and kick the Stanley Cup into the canal. No sooner dared than done — the Cup was booted into the canal. The next day, when questions were raised as to the Cup's whereabouts, a couple of the Ottawa players had to hurry back to the canal and retrieve the snow-covered trophy.

## Stop that thief!

A fan once tried to steal the Stanley Cup in the middle of a play-off game in Chicago. The Montreal Canadiens were suffering through a losing game to the Black Hawks in 1961. The Cup, ready for presentation to the winning team, was on display in a glass case in the lobby of the Chicago Stadium. When it appeared that Chicago would win, a Montreal fan left his seat, rushed into the lobby and smashed the glass case. He threw the Stanley Cup over his shoulder and headed for the nearest exit. He was almost in the clear when some startled ushers and a policeman took up the chase and grabbed him. In court the next day, the thief explained that he was simply trying to take the Cup back to Montreal where it belonged.

## All right, who forgot the Cup?

The Cup-champion Montreal Canadiens were on their way to a victory party in 1924 when they had to stop to fix a flat tire. The players piled out to help make repairs. In doing so, they placed the Stanley Cup on the curb. Moments later, spare tire in place, the players took off to the party ... without the Cup! When they discovered the trophy was missing, they rushed back to search for it. Sure enough, it was still on the curb, right where they had left it.

## The missing collar

Thieves broke into the Hockey Hall of Fame in Toronto in 1970 and stole the original collar off the Cup. The collar was engraved with the names of early champions. The thieves were never caught but the collar turned up seven years later in a Toronto parking lot.

## Guy Lafleur grabs the Cup

Superstar Guy Lafleur quietly slipped away from a Montreal victory party in 1979 with the Stanley Cup. He stuffed it in the trunk of his car and drove to his parents' home in Thurso, Quebec. He placed it on the front lawn and people came from great distances to see the famous trophy and have their pictures taken with it. When Guy wasn't watching, his son began filling the Cup with water from the garden hose. Meanwhile, back in Montreal, officials were searching frantically for the missing trophy.

# AND THE WINNER IS ...

By now, you know the most important team trophy awarded in the NHL is the Stanley Cup, which goes to the winning team after the final game of the play-offs. The Montreal Canadiens have won this trophy a record 23 times.

But there are plenty of other trophies to be won by individual stars, awarded for everything from good sportsmanship to best goaltending. Here's a run-down of some of the most prestigious awards.

- It's a great honour to win the Hart Trophy, awarded annually to the player judged to be most valuable to his team. Wayne Gretzky has won this trophy more often than any other player in NHL history.

- The Calder Memorial Trophy goes to the outstanding rookie in the NHL each season. Players Mario Lemieux, Joe Nieuwendyk and Luc Robitaille are former winners of this trophy. Nieuwendyk is one of only two rookies to score more than 50 goals in his first NHL season. Mike Bossy, the rookie record holder, had 53.

- The player voted best defenceman in the NHL receives the Norris Trophy. Bobby Orr, during his glory years with the Boston Bruins, is the only player to have won this trophy eight times.

- The top goalie in the NHL is rewarded with the Vezina Trophy. Former Montreal Canadiens' goalie Jacques Plante captured this trophy seven times for the record.

- The Bill Masterton Memorial Trophy goes to the player who displays qualities of perseverance, sportsmanship and dedication to hockey.

- The Frank J. Selke Trophy is reserved for the forward who excels in the defensive aspects of the game. Former Montreal star Bob Gainey was awarded this trophy in four consecutive seasons from 1978 to 1981.

- The Conn Smythe Trophy goes to the most valuable player to his team in the Stanley Cup play-offs.

- The Art Ross Trophy goes to the player who leads the league in scoring. Wayne Gretzky won this trophy seven straight times from 1981 to 1987; he's the only player to have done so.

- A season of good, clean play and gentlemanly conduct is recognized with the awarding of the Lady Byng Memorial Trophy. Former New York Islander star Mike Bossy won this award three times during his career.

## Did you know?

- No goalie has ever won the Lady Byng Trophy for clean play and gentlemanly conduct.

- After the New York Rangers' Frank Boucher won the Lady Byng Trophy seven times in eight years, he was allowed to keep it permanently, and a new trophy was made up.

- Bobby Orr is the only defenceman to win the Art Ross Trophy as NHL scoring champion — and he did it twice.

# GAME DAY

If you play hockey, you probably get at least a little anxious on the day of a game — every hockey player does. Professional players are no different. Game day is exciting, and it can mean a lot, not only to the team, but to a player's career as well. Let's follow a pro on game day to see what it's really like.

**8:00 A.M.** I wake up and have a big breakfast and read the newspapers to catch up on all the news from games played the night before.

**9:00 A.M.** I leave for the arena. Because it's a game day, our team will be on the ice first, then the visiting team will skate.

**9:30 A.M.** In the dressing room, I check my equipment. While we get our equipment on, the team discusses our opponents in the game that night. We talk about who's been hurt and who's been playing well.

**10:30 A.M.** We're on the ice warming up. It's not like a practice day when we don't have a game. On those days we work really hard, working on our shots, our passes and line rushes. We practise our power play and penalty killing. On game-day practices — or "skates" — we take shots at our goalies and pass the puck around. The coach may ask for a few line rushes. We skate just hard enough to sweat, but not so hard that we'll be drained of energy for the game.

**11:30 A.M.** After practice, the trainer gives me a massage to loosen up the shoulder I injured in a game a few weeks ago. I shower and read my fan mail. A couple of reporters and the

colour commentator from TV are in the dressing room asking questions. I tell them my sore shoulder is okay and how much I enjoy playing with my new linemates.

**2:30 P.M.** At home again, I have a big pre-game meal with lots of carbohydrates for energy, and quick pre-game nap.

**5:00 P.M.** I drive back to the arena taking the same route I always do — for luck — and park in my lucky parking space.

**5:30 P.M.** Back in the dressing room, I check my sticks. I'm very fussy about my sticks and always make sure they are curved and taped just the way I like them. I have my skates sharpened before every game and sometimes between periods, too.

**6:30 P.M.** The coach holds a short team meeting, to go over the strategy for tonight's game — what to look for, power play set-ups, how we're going to kill penalties — and gives us a pep talk.

**7:25 P.M.** The teams skate onto the ice for the pre-game warmup, which lasts about 20 minutes. The warmup involves a lot of skating, stretching and loosening up. The

back-up goalie stands in the net and handles a lot of shots. When he is warmed up, he gives way to the starting goalie. The warmup is the time when more than 40 players — 20 or more from each team — are on the ice at the same time. Often we'll sneak glances at the players on the other team, sizing them up for the game ahead.

**7:45 P.M.** There's a 15-minute intermission between the warmup and the game while the Zamboni comes on to resurface the ice. I take care of some last-minute stick taping and check my skate laces. A buzzer goes off to tell us when to get back out onto the ice.

**8:05 P.M.** After the starting lineups are announced and the national anthem is played, the puck is finally dropped. The game itself is a blur of furious action. Players charge into each other, take frantic shots, change lines and cheer each other on. I feel great in this game

and full of energy. I score two goals, which gives me even more energy! The team's really playing well tonight and we win 4-3.

**10:30 P.M.** After the game, I'm interviewed on TV because I was selected as one of the three stars of the game. I talk to the newspaper sports writers for a few minutes then get back to the dressing room to shower. Wow, am I hungry! A bunch of us go out to relax and have our post-game meal. The visiting players aren't so lucky — they have a bus waiting to take them to the airport. By 1:00 A.M., I'm exhausted and head home to get some sleep for the big practice we've got tomorrow.

# POWER FOOD

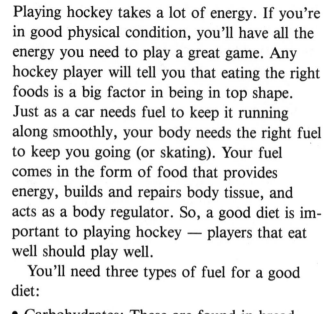

Playing hockey takes a lot of energy. If you're in good physical condition, you'll have all the energy you need to play a great game. Any hockey player will tell you that eating the right foods is a big factor in being in top shape. Just as a car needs fuel to keep it running along smoothly, your body needs the right fuel to keep you going (or skating). Your fuel comes in the form of food that provides energy, builds and repairs body tissue, and acts as a body regulator. So, a good diet is important to playing hockey — players that eat well should play well.

You'll need three types of fuel for a good diet:

• Carbohydrates: These are found in bread, fruits and vegetables, rice, pasta and potatoes.

## Diet tips for hockey players:

• Drink lots of water before, during and after a game or practice. Players often sweat as much as a few litres of water during a strenuous game or practice. The loss of a large amount of water can lead to dehydration — which brings on cramps and muscle weakness.

Carbohydrates are our major and most efficient energy source, so it's important to eat lots every day to fuel our muscles.

• Proteins: Found in lean meat, fish, eggs, poultry, milk, cheese and beans, proteins are the building blocks of the body. To build muscle and maintain good muscle tone you'll need to have some protein in your diet every day.

• Fats: Found in butter, meat, nuts, milk and cheese, fats provide our body with energy as carbohydrates do. But, because our bodies can store fat, we don't need to eat large quantities of it.

A good pre-game power meal might consist of a glass of milk, a salad, spaghetti, some bread and a fruit salad for dessert. Just remember the key to good nutrition — and good hockey playing — is a balanced diet including the three stars of the game — carbohydrates, proteins and fats.

• Don't skip breakfast. A good breakfast supplies much of the fuel your body uses in a day.

• A pre-game meal should be eaten two or three hours before the game. If you skip your pre-game meal, you may not play well because your empty stomach may create hunger pangs. Also, your body's store of glucose may be used up before the game is over, making you tire easily.

# THE ROAD TO THE PROS

Have you ever dreamed of being a professional hockey player? Lots of kids have that dream, but the road that takes you from your first team to a professional hockey team can be a long one — with many obstacles along the way. Players should know what's ahead for them in hockey — and why the road to the pros is like climbing a mountain. It's a lot of fun at first when the trail is a gentle slope — but the higher you climb, the more difficult it becomes. Only the most determined and the most skilful press on to the pros.

On these pages you'll find the ten steps most players encounter on the road that leads to the pros.

After travelling the road that leads to the pros for a number of years, many young players drop out for various reasons. Some players decide that professional hockey just isn't for them, and they pursue another career. Many players are aware that they lack the skills to become NHL players and they may get involved in other sports. Others become more involved in school or hobbies, and some have simply had their fill of organized hockey after 10 or 12 years of games and practices.

It's important to set realistic goals for yourself in hockey. (Statistics tell us fewer less than 1% of all hockey players in Canada turn professional — so the chances of any player becoming a star in the NHL are very slim.) The bottom line is always to make sure you're playing because you're having fun. And a daydream or two about scoring the winning goal in the Stanley Cup play-offs never hurt anyone.

**Step 3:** Atom. For players 10-11.

**Step 2:** Novice. For players up to nine.

**Step 1:** Entry level hockey. Most young players begin playing some form of organized hockey at the age of five, six or seven. The players are often called "tykes" or "mites" and the emphasis is on skill development and fun. This level of hockey prepares a player for all the steps that follow.

**Step 4:** Pee Wee. For players 12-13.
**Step 5:** Bantam. For players up to 15.

**Step 6:** Midget. For players up to 17.
**Step 7:** Juvenile. For players up to 19.

**Step 8:** Junior hockey (A, B, C and D). For players up to 21.
**Step 9:** Major junior A. For players up to 21.

**Step 10:** Professional hockey. Minor pro and the NHL.

# How players get drafted

The biggest day of the year for many young amateur stars occurs in June when the NHL holds its annual entry draft. Throughout the season, the pro teams have been scouting amateur players all over the world — in the junior leagues, in university hockey and throughout Europe. NHL teams also rely on the league's own scouting bureau, Central Scouting, for reliable information on star players.

The teams draft in reverse order to the way they finished in the standings in the previous season. For example, in 1984, the Pittsburgh Penguins finished in last place overall and, with first draft choice, were able to draft Mario Lemieux, who became a superstar.

Although dozens of players are drafted each year, only the top choices are talented enough to step right into major league hockey. The majority of the players drafted spend at least a season or two playing for farm teams in the minor leagues.

How important is the annual entry draft? It's all-important. Teams that draft well fare well. Teams that misjudge the talent available in the draft and make poor selections are often the same teams that struggle to make the play-offs.

# HOCKEY'S HILARIOUS HISTORY

Hockey has changed a lot over the years, and some of hockey's history seems pretty strange to us today. Take a look at this scene. This was what a professional hockey game might have looked like in the early 1900s.

Some early day goaltenders wore peaked caps or hats during games, not just to keep their heads warm but to protect them from fans who brought pea-shooters to the arena. Goalies were a favourite target.

If you were a spectator at an early hockey game, you might get more excitement than you wanted — the boards surrounding the rink weren't very high. Not only did fans duck flying pucks but quite often players were dumped into the crowd, landing in the laps of the spectators.

In hockey's early days, players were often presented with a bouquet of flowers if they starred in a game. Today's game stars win trophies, gifts and cash awards.

In the 1920s, most players on a team played the full 60 minutes (today's players play about 20 minutes). In those days, each team carried only two or three substitutes. In Ottawa one season, when mid-winter temperatures in the Ottawa Arena dropped well below freezing, substitutes on the Ottawa bench retired to their dressing room where they gathered round the stove and played cards. If the coach needed one of the subs, he pushed a buzzer at the bench and one of the players hurried out.

In the early days, goal judges stood out on the ice behind the net. They wore heavy coats and boots to keep warm and waved a handkerchief or a flag to signal a goal. Quite often they had to leap out of the way when the play swirled in behind the goal.

It used to be that hockey players would have regular day jobs as well as playing hockey. Goalie Guy Fournier of the Buckingham, Quebec, team was ready for the opening whistle one night when he heard the town fire alarm go off. Fournier raced from the arena, still wearing his skates and pads. After helping his father, the fire chief, put out a blaze in a nearby department store, Fournier returned to the arena and helped his team to a 4-1 victory.

# THE HOCKEY HALL OF FAME

Where would you find the Chicoutimi Cucumber, Jake the Snake, the Golden Jet or the Stratford Streak? In the Hockey Hall of Fame, of course. Since it opened in Toronto in 1961, several million hockey fans have strolled through the shrine that honours hockey's greatest stars and the deeds they accomplished. Let's take a trip through the hall and see a few of the highlights.

Who does this tiny pair of skates belong to? They're the first skates worn by Wayne Gretzky. And here are the battered skates worn by speedy Howie Morenz, who was known as the Stratford Streak. There are the goal skates worn by former Canadien goalie Georges Vezina, the pride of Chicoutimi, Quebec. Vezina was so cool in goal he earned the nickname the Chicoutimi Cucumber.

Equally cool at puckstopping was Jacques Plante, another former Canadien, whose nickname was Jake the Snake. Plante's catching hand would flick out to snare pucks the way a snake's tongue would flick out to trap insects. Plante's first crude face mask is here too.

Among the many sticks in the Hall is one Bobby (the Golden Jet) Hull used to blast in so many goals. It has a fiercely hooked blade that wouldn't be legal today. Now there are restrictions on the curvature of a stick blade. Over there's the ancient goal stick oldtime netminder Percy Lesueur used in every game for five consecutive seasons.

There are hundreds of photographs in the hall, dozens of trophies, medals, mementos and even a movie theatre. And of course, you can't leave without seeing the Stanley Cup.

## Deciding who gets in ...

How does a player become accepted into the Hockey Hall of Fame? Players are elected by a jury made up of former players, media members and hockey executives. Three players are inducted each year and there's special recognition for game officials, builders of the game and members of the media. Only a small percentage of all players are inducted — so it's a great honour to be included. For most players, joining the other hockey legends in the Hall of Fame is even better than the thrill of winning a Stanley Cup.

Over here is a battered puck. It's the only puck known to have survived a full NHL game (Los Angeles at Minnesota, November 10, 1979). In an average game, the puck is replaced every few minutes, usually after it's shot or deflected into the crowd. And look, there's the puck Canadian astronaut Marc Garneau carried with him into space — he must have thought a hockey puck was a good symbol of Canada.

83

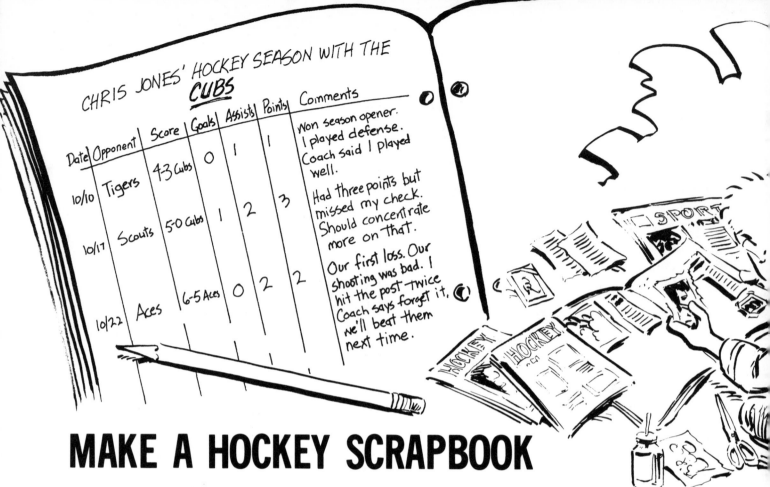

CHRIS JONES' HOCKEY SEASON WITH THE **CUBS**

| Date | Opponent | Score | Goals | Assists | Points | Comments |
|------|----------|-------|-------|---------|--------|----------|
| 10/10 | Tigers | 4-3 Cubs | 0 | 1 | 1 | Won season opener. I played defense. Coach said I played well. |
| 10/17 | Scouts | 5-0 Cubs | 1 | 2 | 3 | Had three points but missed my check. Should concentrate more on that. |
| 10/22 | Aces | 6-5 Aces | 0 | 2 | 2 | Our first loss. Our shooting was bad. I hit the post twice. Coach says forget it. We'll beat them next time. |

# MAKE A HOCKEY SCRAPBOOK

If you play hockey, if you're a hockey fan, or if you have one favourite player, then a scrapbook is for you. It's great for collecting hockey photographs, clippings and articles and any other hockey memorabilia you can find that reflects your interest in the game. It's also a good way to keep a record of your own progress as a player. It's something you can keep forever, and it'll be fun to look back through your scrapbook years from now. If you don't already have a scrapbook, it's never too late to start one. Here are some suggestions to help you get started.

Decide what you want to keep in your scrapbook. You can cut out articles and pictures of your favourite team or player from newspapers and magazines (make sure everyone's read them first). Or keep track of important hockey events that happen throughout the season. Why not write a letter to the team or player you admire most? Many hockey teams are good about getting back to their fans.

If you know you are going to meet a sports celebrity at a sports banquet or in a shopping mall, why not get a friend to take your photograph with the celebrity? It'll add a really personal touch to your scrapbook. When you tape or paste a photo or a clipping in your scrapbook, write a short paragraph under it stating why it's included, why you chose to keep it.

If you play hockey, keep a scrapbook about your own life and adventures. You can keep a game-by-game account of your season. Set it up something like the example on page 84 and include scores of games, personal goals and assists as well as your own summary of the games played. At the end of the schedule, write your account of the season in your scrapbook and don't forget to include any team pictures and crests you received.

# Hockey cards

Do you collect hockey bubblegum cards? Many fans say they first became interested in hockey because of the popular cards.

Card collectors can trace their hobby back to 1910 when the first cards were issued by cigarette companies. By 1923, at least four candy manufacturers jumped on the hockey bandwagon and began distributing cards.

In the 1930s, the St. Lawrence Starch Co. began distributing hockey photos of Maple Leaf and Canadien players. By 1939, players from all six of the NHL teams could be collected. All you had to do was strip off the label of a tin of corn syrup and mail it in. In the return mail would be a photo of one of your favourite players.

The corn syrup promotion was suspended in 1968 after the NHL demanded more and more money for the rights to the players' photos. Today a full set of corn syrup hockey photos, in good condition, would be worth thousands of dollars.

To most people, hockey cards are merely a small piece of cardboard with a photo of a player on the front and some career statistics on the back. But to a serious collector, cards are something to be cherished. They're fun to trade, too. The bubblegum that comes with them is gone in minutes but the cards will last a lifetime.

# THE GREAT HOCKEY QUIZ

Once you've read this book, you should be able to score well on the great hockey quiz. Fifteen or more correct answers makes you an All Star. Get fewer than five answers correct and you're assigned to the minor leagues. Check the answers on page 91 to see where you stand.

1. What man gave his name to hockey's oldest trophy?
   a. Gordie Howe
   b. Clarence Campbell
   c. Lord Stanley

2. Who invented the machine that resurfaces ice, making it fresh and smooth for skaters?
   a. King Clancy
   b. Abby Hoffman
   c. Frank Zamboni

3. Which NHL team has won the most Stanley Cups?
   a. Toronto Maple Leafs
   b. Montreal Canadiens
   c. Boston Bruins

4. Who holds the NHL record for most career points?
   a. Rocket Richard
   b. Wayne Gretzky
   c. Bobby Hull

5. Which NHL trophy can a player win only once in his career?
   a. Smythe
   b. Art Ross
   c. Calder

6. Which NHL trophy goes to the most valuable player in the play-offs?
   a. Norris
   b. Smythe
   c. Hart

7. How many regular season games does each NHL team play?
   a. 60
   b. 70
   c. 80

8. Name the most important skill for hockey players to master.
   a. passing
   b. shooting
   c. skating

9. Name the player who was still playing in the NHL when he was 50 years old.
   a. Gordie Howe
   b. Phil Esposito
   c. Bobby Hull

10. In the 1970s, a defenceman won the NHL scoring title twice. Can you name him?
    a. Borje Salming
    b. Bobby Orr
    c. Serge Savard

11. You are on a breakaway when you are tripped from behind by an opposing player. The referee awards you a free shot at the goalie. What is this shot called?

12. After 60 minutes of play in a regular season game, the score is tied and the teams play another short period of five minutes or less. What is this extra period called?

13. The final score is 2-0. What has the winning goalie earned?

14. The linesman catches you skating over the blue line ahead of the puck, which is being passed to you by a teammate. What does he call?

15. Where is the puck dropped to start the game?

16. Who is the man in charge on the ice?

17. What is a first-year player called?

18. If you get a major penalty, how many minutes must you spend in the penalty box?

19. What do you call a player who is elected to be team spokesman?

20. If the team you're playing against has a player in the penalty box, what kind of a play does your team have going?

# FIFTY YEARS IN HOCKEY

How many people can say they've skated with or against such hockey superstars as Cyclone Taylor (who played back in the early 1900s), Gordie Howe, Rocket Richard or Bobby Hull, as well as some of today's best players such as Wayne Gretzky and Mario Lemieux? The author of this book can. Brian McFarlane has been on the ice with many of hockey's biggest names, either holding a hockey stick or a microphone in front of him. You've probably seen Brian McFarlane on TV as an announcer — he's been with Hockey Night in Canada for over 25 years.

Growing up in Ottawa, Brian played hockey well enough to be on a junior A team for three years. During the playoffs in his final season of junior hockey, he was called to check superstar Jean Beliveau. "I couldn't stop Beliveau," he recalls. "And I decided right then that I wouldn't make it to the NHL as a player. But perhaps there'd be room for me in the broadcast booth."

## As All America centre set scoring records

After his final junior season, Brian accepted a scholarship to St. Lawrence University in Canton, New York. There he became an All America centre and set scoring records that still stand today. As team captain, he twice led

Brian McFarlane on the Hockey Night in Canada set with Mario Lemieux

St. Lawrence to the U.S. College hockey championship tournament. A top student, he was president of his class for three years. He took courses in radio and television and did play-by-play of the college football and baseball games.

## Broadcasting career began during summer holidays

Brian's professional broadcasting career began at radio station CFRA in Ottawa during summer holidays while he was still in college. After graduation in 1955, he became a television sportscaster in Schenectady, New York, and two years later moved back to Canada and joined radio station CFRB in Toronto.

Brian became the first Canadian hockey commentator to appear on U.S. network telecasts in 1960, when he did between-period interviews for the CBS network.

One year, the NHL Oldtimers in Toronto needed an extra player and they asked Brian if he'd play right wing for them. He was the only amateur player on the team and for the next 17 years he played hundreds of games with the Oldtimers.

"I was living the dream of every amateur player in Canada," says McFarlane of his experience playing with the many Hockey Hall of Famers on the Oldtimers team.

"One night we played a team of media all-stars, and the media team introduced a skinny 11-year-old. We let the kid skate right between our defence once or twice and he scored a couple of goals. The kid's name was Wayne Gretzky. What great moves he had — even at that age."

Brian calls Gretzky the most exciting player he's ever seen, although he says, "Bobby Orr and Gordie Howe are also tops on my list."

During his 25 years with Hockey Night in Canada, Brian's witnessed many changes in the game he loves.

"When I started broadcasting hockey games there were only six teams in the NHL, and each team carried just one goalie. That meant the seventh best goalie in the world was in the minors. If a goalie was injured during a game, a standby goalie sitting in the stands would hurry down to the dressing room for a quick change and take over. Or perhaps the trainer on the team would volunteer to put on the pads.

"When I began, most goalies refused to wear face masks, claiming they couldn't see the puck well enough through the mask. There were no names on the backs of jerseys and the average player's salary was about $16,000 per season. There were no replays of goals on television and no highlights of games played in other cities."

## Writing runs in the McFarlane family

Over the years Brian has written over 30 books on hockey. His first novel for young people is titled *The Youngest Goalie*. Writing runs in the McFarlane family. Brian's father was the original author of the Hardy Boys books, writing under the name Franklin W. Dixon. His father also wrote some exciting hockey stories, perhaps that's what first got Brian interested in the game. If so, it's an interest that has continued to grow over the years.

89

**Permissions**

"The secret of the stars", pages 40-41, from *How Sport Works: An Ontario Science Centre Book*. Text copyright ©1988 by The Centennial Centre of Science and Technology. Reprinted by permission of Kids Can Press Ltd.


**Photo Credits**

Page 8:  Bruce Bennett Studios
Page 15: Photo Turofsky, from the author's collection
Page 19: Photograph by F. Lennon, from The Toronto Star
Page 37: The Globe and Mail
Page 59: City of Edmonton Archives, from the author's collection
Page 60: Smiths and Clayton Photographers, courtesy of
        Samantha Holmes
Page 62: Photograph by Robert B. Shaver, from the author's collection
Page 63: Photograph by Michael Burns, from the author's collection
Page 64: Photograph by Robert B. Shaver, from the author's collection
Page 66: Ten-year-old Gretzky, from the author's collection
Page 66: Gretzky with L.A. Kings, Bruce Bennett Studios
Page 88: From the author's collection

# ANSWERS

The great hockey quiz, p. 86

| | |
|---|---|
| 1.c | 11. a penalty shot |
| 2.c | 12. overtime |
| 3.b | 13. a shut-out |
| 4.b | 14. you are offside |
| 5.c | 15. at centre ice |
| 6.b | 16. the referee |
| 7.c | 17. a rookie |
| 8.c | 18. five minutes |
| 9.a | 19. a captain |
| 10.b | 20. power play |

# GLOSSARY

**Assist:** a point credited to a player in the individual scoring race when the player helps set up a goal by a teammate.

**Backhand:** a shot taken from the "wrong side." For a right-hand shooter, the shot would be taken from the left side of the body, using the "back side" of the stick blade.

**Breakaway:** when the puck carrier has just one defender — the goalie — to beat.

**Captain:** sometimes appointed by management, more often elected by his teammates, the team captain is the only player allowed to discuss issues with a game official. The captain always has the letter "C" stitched on his jersey.

**Checking:** using your body or stick to block or interfere with an opponent. It's legal when an opponent has the puck or was the last player to touch it.

**Close-checking:** describes a game in which teams guard or check their opponents closely and there are few scoring opportunities ("a close-checking game").

**Crease:** the 1.2 m (4 foot) by 2.4 m (8 foot) area in front of the goal occupied by the goaltender.

**Farm team:** the minor league affiliate of an NHL team.

**Goal:** a goal is credited to a player who shoots the puck into the opposing team's net, or to an offensive player who last touched the puck before a defensive player deflected it into his own net. The puck must be fully over the goal line before a goal is signalled.

**Goal nets:** the goal nets are each 1.2 m (4 feet) high, anchored by magnetic fixtures screwed into the rink floor. The crossbar is 1.8 m long, creating a 1.2 m (4 feet) by 1.8 m (6 feet) scoring area. The net is made of white nylon cord, laced around a heavy canvas material at the bottom frame of the goal. The crossbar and posts are painted red.

**Minors:** the minors are the lower levels of professional hockey such as the American Hockey League and the International Hockey League.

**Point man:** a player on the attacking team (usually a defenceman) who takes up a position just inside the opposing team's blue line. This helps to keep the puck in the opposing team's zone and sets the point man up for a shot on goal.

**Power play:** a situation in which a team has a one- or two-player advantage when the opposing team has a player or players in the penalty box.

**Rookie:** a player competing in his first season with a team.

**Save:** a stop by a goalie to prevent a score. A busy goalie may make 30 to 50 saves in a game.

**Shut-out:** when one team stops the other team from scoring for the full 60 minutes of a game. The winning team's goalie is credited with a shut-out in the goaltending statistics.

**Slot:** the area in front of the goal from which players have the best chance of scoring.

**Slump:** describes a period when a player or team is not doing well. The player does not perform up to his capabilities, or the team fails to win.

**Time clock:** an electrical clock whose purpose is to accurately inform officials, players and spectators of the time remaining in a game and the time remaining in any penalties.

**Upstairs:** to shoot the puck high into the top part of the goal net means to put it "upstairs."

**Zones:** the three playing zones on the ice are the attacking (or offensive) zone, neutral zone and defending (or defensive) zone. The NHL adopted the three zones in 1918.

# INDEX